MW00904926

# *The Ultimate College Relationship Guide*

*How to Distinguish Between Love and Drama*

Spiritual and Psychological Guidance to Releasing Negative
Relationship Patterns and Attracting Emotionally Healthy and Loving
Partners

Nancy Pina
Relationship Expert & Advisor

Copyright 2006 by Nancy Pina

The Ultimate College Relationship Guide
How to Distinguish Between Love and Drama

Copyright 2006 by Nancy Pina

ISBN: 1-931947-18-X


Cover Design by Nancy Pina

ALL RIGHTS RESERVED

No part of this publication may be reproduced, stored in a retrieval system, or transmitted, in any form or by any means (electronic, mechanical, photocopying, recording or otherwise) without prior written permission.

The names of the individuals depicted in this book have been changed to protect their identity.

For information, contact:

Nancy Pina

Email: nancyp@yourtruematch.com

Scripture quotations marked "AMP" are from the Amplified® Bible, Copyright © 1954, 1958, 1962, 1964, 1965, 1987 by The Lockman Foundation. Used by permission.

Scripture quotations marked "NKJV" are taken from the New King James Version, Copyright © 1982 by Thomas Nelson Inc. Used by permission. All rights reserved.

Scripture quotations marked "NLT" are taken from the Holy Bible, New Living Translation, copyright 1996. Used by permission of Tyndale House Publishers, Inc. Wheaton, Illinois 60189. All rights reserved.

# Dedication

This book is dedicated to my wonderful and beloved husband Blas. God truly blessed my life the day we met and each day thereafter.

I love you so much, my love of my life and I can't imagine life without you.

I humbly give God all the glory as it is only by His grace and divine wisdom I could write this book;

The credit goes to you dear reader for taking this brave step towards manifesting emotionally healthy relationships;

And lastly, the pleasure has been mine in assisting you on this magnificent journey to true love.

I will bless the Lord at all times;
His praise shall continually be in my mouth.

My soul shall make its boast in the Lord;
The humble shall hear of it and be glad.

Oh, magnify the Lord with me,
And let us exalt His name together.

I sought the Lord, and He heard me,
And delivered me from all my fears.

They looked to Him and were radiant,
And their faces were not ashamed.

This poor man cried out, and the Lord heard him,
And saved him out of all his troubles.

The angel of the Lord encamps all around those who fear Him,
And delivers them.

Oh, taste and see that the Lord is good;
Blessed is the man who trusts in Him!

Oh, fear the Lord, you His saints!

There is no want to those who fear Him.

The young lions lack and suffer hunger;
But those who seek the Lord shall not lack any good thing. Psalm 34:1-10(NKJV)

# Foreword

Although the book title may imply it is primarily for women, I assure you that men are struggling just as much in their search for the right relationship partner. The challenges you face in your intimate relationships may have you feeling somewhat isolated. The good news is there is a reason why certain patterns repeat - and you do have the power to change. Intimate relationships can have a positive or negative impact on your mental, emotional and physical well being. No one teaches Relationship 101, so I personally want to help you navigate through relationship landmines you may encounter during your college years and beyond and teach you practical steps to overcome those obstacles.

The trap of becoming involved with someone who emotionally drains your spirit is a very real possibility – and can happen before you know what hit you. No matter what your age, I have discovered that people who have not resolved their past issues and the pain associated with and stemming from former relationships are often attracted to those who ignite their negative beliefs about themselves.

These beliefs are formed early in life, and it is through intimate relationships in particular that we try to resolve those issues. As a former matchmaker, many of my clients were not truly ready for a commitment when they first came to see me because their past issues had not been addressed.

I have included in this book actual stories from women (and men) who have sought my advice since my first book, *The Right Relationship Can Happen,* was published. You will read about the struggles these people have fought over the years and see how patterns develop. You may recognize yourself in these stories, having had similar experiences and feelings. For each issue you will read about, there are countless others who are living through the same type of emotional and spiritual struggle.

One of my goals in this book is teach you how to break free from the bondage of your self-destructive cycles and attract a well adjusted person. Make no mistake, you are in a spiritual battle and it is your bond with God that will give you the strength and wisdom to end your attraction to these individuals.

The primary aspiration of this book is to provide guidance for an honest examination of past choices so you can resolve the issues that blocks stability and draw you closer to God. Overall, it is your relationship with Jesus Christ that will positively impact your choices and your quality of life.

Even though you may not have marriage or even a long term commitment on your mind right now, it is vital that you believe that you possess the capability to attract the right partner and that you are worthy of experiencing true and unshakeable love.

You do not have to settle for a relationship that is unfulfilling and unloving. Life is better shared with the right partner. This should be someone you consider a friend, confidant, and intimate companion and a blessing brought to you by God in His perfect timing.

# Table of Contents

# Part One

---

# Why Are They All Not "The One?

In Part One, Why Are They All Not "The One?" you will read in detail descriptions and personal accounts concerning the four schemas that most commonly affect relationships:

- Abandonment
- Mistrust and Abuse
- Emotional Deprivation
- Unrelenting Standards.

You will read about the emotional struggles of many individuals and may identify with their situation and the types of people they attract. At the end of Part One, you will find helpful exercises to guide you towards identifying which schema(s) apply to you and how and when they originated.

# Chapter One
## How Did I Get Here?

*Different Person, New Hope, Same Pattern, Identical Ending ...Every Time!*

All of us attract partners in accordance with our core, controlling beliefs and life experiences. If you consistently attract emotional unhealthy attachments, there is a pattern that you must break in order to recognize what a balanced and devoted relationship looks and feels like.

Keep in mind that the matters you face are always about the lessons you need to learn and the issues you have to confront. You're not just "unlucky in love," and the good ones aren't all taken.

During my years of matchmaking, I found that relationship struggles are two-fold: a psychological challenge to break free of underlying schemas or controlling beliefs, and a lack of faith and trust in God. Controlling beliefs are difficult to change, as human nature resists change, even if the behavior is self-defeating.

The pattern or theme that starts in childhood and repeats throughout life (until the pattern is broken and resolved) is called a *schema*. Your schemas determine how you think, feel, act and relate to others. Repetition compulsion is what Freud called the phenomenon of why we repeat the pain of our childhood. The young girl who vows never to marry an abusive alcoholic man like her father ends up marrying such a person; the neglected child is most attracted to cold and ambivalent partners as an adult; the emotionally and verbally abused child becomes the ugliness he experienced and inflicts his pain on those he loves most.

By recognizing the personality traits that particular schemas produce, you can start healing from your past pain and learn how to redefine your core beliefs. You can have power over your thoughts and stop allowing your thoughts to be in command of you.

The primary schemas that harm relationships are:

# Abandonment

This is a feeling that the people you love will leave you and you will end up alone forever. However you imagine they will leave, you always have a deep and entrenched feeling that you will end up alone. When your schema is set off, you may find yourself clinging to your partner desperately, which pushes them away. Thus you unconscious belief of abandonment is fulfilled.

# Mistrust and Abuse

You expect that you will be hurt by others somehow. Either they will emotionally hurt you through lies, manipulation, and humiliation – or physically hurt you.

In order to protect yourself from potential harm, you have learned to keep people at a distance. You expect betrayal in your relationships and assume the worst. Your beliefs become a self fulfilling prophecy.

# Emotional Deprivation

You believe no one truly cares about you or really understand you at your core. You are highly attracted to cold relationship partners, who leave you feeling cheated, unsatisfied and lonely.

## Unrelenting Standards

You are driven by worldly status and the trappings of the successful life, defined by society. Money, career achievement, power, and recognition are more important to you than inner happiness. Your high expectations feel natural to you even though they stress you out.

In the following chapters, we will explore these four controlling core schemas, including how each manifestation affects your choices and how to disentangle from the cycle once and for all.

You will read about people who go from one person to the next, frustrated that their relationships all unfold in the same manner. My message to you is that you can free yourself of these patterns and attract an emotionally healthy person. Understanding the psychology behind your choices and patterns is only half the battle. Your relationship problems are a spiritual war as much as a psychological fight.

In essence, you are a compilation of your past experiences, the choices you made, and the paths you followed. The larger question you need to honestly assess is, *"Do I allow my past mistakes, circumstances, and pain to define who I am?"* Are you holding on to sorrow and becoming a person who is identified by that grief? Your past pain is an opportunity to gain wisdom, grow emotionally, and rise to another level of spiritual maturity.

Eleanor Roosevelt said, *"No one can make you feel inferior without your consent."* [i] When your relationships do not work out, do you ask God when is He going to do something to fix the situation? Faith requires us to do what we can first and allow God to work His will for your life.

Sometimes that means a door will close to love which you thought was the door to the love of your life. One of my prayers is to have the wisdom to accept the doors that close, even when I don't understand why they have been shut so that God can open the best ones for my life.

God wants you to take charge of your life and stop being restricted by people and circumstances. When you are betrayed and rejected in love and feel the depths of depression cover your world that is the time to command the darkness to be cast away from your life.

It is the time to declare that you will not be conquered. You are here today because of the decisions you made in the past. If you do not take responsibility for your life and the people you have brought into your life, you will not be able to attract the right person and live gloriously.

When love ends, it is normal to grieve over it for a period of time. However, grieving is a process that does not last forever. A verse in the book of Psalms addresses grieving in this way: *"Weeping may endure for a night, but joy comes in the morning."* Psalm 30:5 (NKJV) There comes a time for you to let the sunshine back into your life and start living again.

Your past can be the bondage that prevents you from reaping the harvest of an affectionate, rewarding and gratifying union. The action you must take consists of reflection, understanding, and forgiveness of the previous choices, along with resolving suppressed issues. These are necessary steps to take to attract this type of relationship. God can do His divine part in freeing your soul from the burden of earlier pain from love if you take the first step toward healing your heart.

By reading this book, you are taking a fundamental step in heeding God's voice commanding you to attack the issues that are trying to destroy your success. He will enable you to conquer your fears by His power.

You are in a spiritual battle that requires you to do your part and allow God to do His part. If you don't work through these issues and deal with your past sorrow, you will continue to attract the same type of individuals into your life.

The deception of self-help is its incompleteness. You cannot completely heal and forgive others without the divine help of God. If you understand the human *why* in your life, but leave out the divine, you will continually be spiritually needy and unfulfilled. Understanding your past will get you on the road to freedom from its repression.

Sometimes God has to take someone away from you before you can see what He has for you in His perfect plan. You will never find your divine relationship if you seek the easy way and allow people to float in and out of your life. You can't run away from the circumstances and issues that God continually brings into your life to conquer and overcome.

You have the power to free yourself from the obstacle of former love cycles and turn it into an opportunity for success. The key is your fortitude, which will turn these issues into blessings. Adversity is prosperity to those who have resilience. There is always a struggle before success, especially in love.

Sometimes pride can prevent you from taking the road to healing. Your mind may tell you that the other person is the one with the problems. But that is pride affecting your thoughts and ultimately your future. Pride will block your perception of why you have attracted certain individuals and cloud your mind with lies and excuses.

Pride is an exaggerated opinion of oneself, blinded to self-destructive behaviors but openly mindful and critical of others who show a prideful attitude. Pride is a true spiritual adversary, and it will destroy you if you do not get rid of it.

The first step to free yourself from this bondage involves understanding the psychological reasons you attract the partners you do. There are specific causes for why you are strongly attracted to people who are damaging to you.

You attract destructive partners because the interaction you have with them brings about feelings from your childhood. These feelings are your controlling beliefs, and those unhealthy emotions are soothing to you because you are accustomed to them and equate intimacy with those feelings.

By unconsciously attracting certain individuals, you create situations similar to what you experienced early in life. Thus, you react in the same manner as you did as a child, oftentimes with more intensity. When those buttons are pushed, you unconsciously react to a past event and not to the current situation with your present partner.

Almost all suppressed pain and hurtful feelings are a result of upbringing issues and disappointments you have not come to terms with in the present. They still drive and control your relationships. These events form fundamental core beliefs and impact your intimate life. To break free of old patterns, you must go back and look at your past relationships and understand why these circumstances unfolded.

By taking responsibility for the choices you have made, and not casting blame on others, you are one step closer to attracting the right partner.

# Chapter Two
## One Day You Will Leave Me Too

### *Why Emotionally Unavailable People Are Appealing*

In dating situations:

- Are you drawn to those who are unavailable to you in some significant way?
- Have you been attracted to married people or those who are in committed relationships with someone else?
- Are you drawn to individuals who have limited time for you, such as workaholics, long-distance relationships, chat room only relationships, or people who travel all the time?
- Have you seriously dated people who treated you with ambivalence?

If you believe the people you love will leave, and you will end up emotionally isolated, a fear of abandonment dictates your behavior. You feel that you will be left alone, whether the people close to you die, leave home forever, or walk out on you for someone else. Because of this core belief, you may cling too much and end up pushing people away. Even normal, brief partings may upset you.

Abandonment anxiety begins early in life and involves basic safety. While growing up, you may have experienced a turbulent family environment and felt vulnerable, fragile, and moody. You probably felt that something terrible might happen at any moment. Those who were supposed to love, care, and protect you did not, which resulted in a feeling of desertion.

Because of this pattern, you are drawn to people who have the potential to trigger this feeling of abandonment. You may be attracted to those who seem to have the potential to provide you with stability, but never completely fulfill it. Your partners keep you guessing about their level of commitment to you.

Because this is a familiar feeling, you are attracted to the idea of never really being sure if they will remain in your life.

## Why Can't I Be a Top Priority?

Take, for example, a young woman named Linda, whose abandonment issues have manifested in her current relationship. She writes:

> *I am in a relationship with an older guy. He treats me great, except that he never wants to go on a date. All it seems like he wants to do is stay at home and watch movies. The last time I asked him to take me out he said he didn't have enough money to take me out. Later that night he went to a bar with a friend. It always seems like he's ditching me for this same friend.*

> *When my boyfriend goes off with his friend, I always get jealous and mad, but I don't know why. I'm also very insecure, because we have a ten year age difference. I'm scared he'll cheat on me, even though he says he won't.*

> *I believe him, but when he goes to the bar, I just get very upset. What should I*

*do? Why do I keep getting jealous and angry? Could you please help me?*

Because of her fundamental beliefs, Linda allows her boyfriend to treat her disrespectfully. She does not believe that she deserves to be respected or loved by a man who will be grateful to have her in his life. You may have experienced a similar type of relationship.

Core beliefs form early in life, and left unattended they will unconsciously prevail over present relationships. Linda formed a primary belief that men will cheat and leave her. Her father left her mother when Linda was a teenager and openly cheated on her before they finally divorced.

His emotional and physical absence from her life caused her great insecurity as a child and continues to plague her as an adult. She has not consciously acknowledged the abandonment she felt when her father left her family or how painful that experience was for her.

She has not made the connection between her anger towards her father and the type of men she attracts. She continually manifests relationships that bring this feeling of abandonment to the surface.

One of the first questions Linda must ask herself is what she wants from this man.

- Does she want to get married eventually?
- Does she desire children in the future?
- Does she see the importance of sharing her boyfriend's morals, values, and life goals?

These are important issues to face. There is no reason to settle for someone who does not meet your goals, needs, and desires. If the man in your life does not meet even the basic desire you have for a long-term commitment, you must give yourself permission to end it and be determined in your thoughts and words that the best person is yet to come into your life.

Regardless of her decision to stay or go, it is imperative that Linda address her past and become conscious of her decisions so she may start on the path to healing.

## I Want You All To Myself

If you are insecure about a love relationship and very dependent on your boyfriend or girlfriend, you are likely to be jealous. You may see "signs" of disaster when none are there. Such is the case with Chad who admittedly is very possessive and jealous of his girlfriend. He formed a core belief that the women he loved would eventually leave him after his mother abandoned him as a young child.

He always felt that if he had been better behaved, she would have stayed. Unconsciously, he attracts women who bring this tension in his relationships and is fearful that they will find someone better to be with.

*My name is Chad and I am 21 years old. I was dating my girlfriend for since we were 17 and I am very much in love with her. We were always very close with each other and had seen each other pretty much everyday. She always told me how much she loved me, loved being with me and enjoyed spending time together. We often spoke about marriage in the future and spending our lives together. I always looked forward to having a future with her because she is my best friend and I love her and want to marry her. We always had our share of fights and they were always stupid things.*

*My jealousy and possessiveness started to become a big problem though. I will admit that I am very jealous and always start fights with her when she wants to go to a club with her friends. We started fighting a lot about this and she then broke up with me. I was a mess and I pleaded with her everyday to give me a chance and time to change. I read books about the issues and I also saw a therapist. I called her everyday asking her to try and work things out with me for months and months. I finally stopped and gave her what she wanted and left her alone. I tried moving on with my life. After about a month of us not talking, she began to miss me and would get upset over me.*

*She did not call me and tell me these things but friends of hers did. I also saw her one night at a club and she was crying because we weren't talking. A couple weeks later, she found out I started seeing someone. Then she began calling me crying about how much she misses me and wants to be together and how she made a mistake. I was reluctant at first to believe her and was scared that I was setting myself up to be hurt again.*

*As much as I tried not to get back with her I couldn't resist. I hated seeing her crying and upset and a big part of me did want her back. We got back together and this was a little over a month ago and now she broke up with me again. She says I still haven't changed and that she is unhappy. I want nothing more than to make her happy and happy with me. I am*

21

*so sick of the club scene and just want an
adult relationship where the focus is on
the relationship and spending time together. I don't know what to do anymore
and I miss her so much. Can you please
help me with your advice? Do you think
this is it for good? I love her very much
and really do not want to lose her for
good.*

Chad's relationship issues are still present because he has not made
peace with his mother's abandonment. Once he releases his unwar-
ranted guilt of her actions, he will no longer be attracted to women
who create this tension.

## I Know It Will Be Different This Time

Our minds can delude us into believing we have found the love of our
life. We later realize all we really did was attract the same type of
destructive relationship partner we've had before.

Gregg wrote to me about his girlfriend and the unresolved problems she
has with her ex-boyfriend and his difficulties with his father. His story
exemplifies how unresolved feelings of abandonment early in life will
continue to lead one to draw the same type of person who ignites those
emotions are addressed and resolved.

*I met this woman, she's 22, and I am 30.
She's mature for her age and is responsible and all that. But, she has some issues
from her past that she needs to deal with.
She has some walls up and doesn't allow
people to get too close. I knew this from
the beginning so we decided to be just
friends and let her deal with her getting
over her ex.*

*Sounds easy enough. However, we have such a connection and we have so much fun together that we started a relationship without even thinking about it. It happened right in front of us. She told me that her walls were coming down with me and she began opening up about things in her past. It's nothing too crazy just things she needs to deal with and she knows it and she wants to take care of them so that maybe in the future we can have something.*

*Now, I also have some issues about my past that I have to deal with. I started going to counseling to deal with the loss of my father and some abandonment issues created way back when I was 12 or 13. Basically we decided we're not ready for a relationship and we both need to deal with these things on our own. My counselor asked me not to have any contact with her AT ALL for a while so I can deal with this issue.*

*Erin and I talked about it and she completely understood because she had just asked me for the same space. The next day she called me from vacation to wish me luck on my exam. It was a nice thing to do but only one day after we said no contact. She then called me two days later just to say hi.*

*Then I went to Florida and I called her a few days later, which I shouldn't have done. She called me a few days later and then when I got home (about 10 days after we decided no contact) she wanted to see me and she slept over. Nothing happened and we did talk about no contact and what we were doing.*

*I guess we just missed each other, it's hard for us. We both want to be together I think but we know we can't right now. So, this is actually the third time we have tried to be just friends. But we both think this time it's different because we finally admit we both have issues we have to deal with. We have set limits. We're not going to be intimate. I'm not going to email her or text messages her AT ALL.*

*Do you see anything happening here? Are we being overly optimistic? Do you think its okay for us to at least try to be friends? I mean, I am taking care of myself and my issue with my Dad right now with counseling and I have made myself a top priority and so has she.*

*Do you think if she was older that it would be easier to stay apart? Is it true that if we really have a connection and are truly meant to be together and that three months of no contact won't harm that? It's just really hard for us not to talk at all and I don't think talking once or twice a week is going to hurt as long as we don't get intimate and just hang out as buddies.*

Gregg's unresolved feeling of abandonment towards his father is magnified because of his sudden death. He unconsciously attracts women who create a similar feeling of abandonment because it is a familiar feeling and he longs for understanding and meaning for what happened in his teenage years.

What makes Gregg's emotional recovery more challenging is the permanent absence of his father and the opportunity he loss to heal while his father was alive.

We are most strongly attracted to those partners who ignite our flawed core beliefs. Because Gregg is in such an emotionally vulnerable place, he must take a step back from all relationships, even the "just friends" relationship he believes he can have with Erin.

Gregg has duplicated a pattern of attracting a woman who is emotionally unavailable who is likely to leave him, in this case because of her own personal insecurities and the age difference. He is automatically most strongly attracted to this type of woman because she ignites the feeling of abandonment he lived through when he was a child.

When Gregg was ten years old, his father was diagnosed with a serious illness and was hospitalized for long periods of time. He was largely kept in the dark about the severity of his illness, as his family thought he was too young to grasp what his father was going through.

Not comprehending what was happening made Gregg even more anxious. His father eventually died several years later—a painful and devastating blow to a young child.

The younger the child, the more potent this issue will be in his or her life as an adult. Because Gregg did not have another stable fraternal figure in his life after this loss, the memory of being abandoned remains as an open wound in his soul.

Until he resolves the problems he has around his childhood abandonment, he will continue to attract women who are unavailable like Erin.

# I Want to Feel Important

If you faced emotional abandonment in your childhood, perhaps from a parent who worked constantly, leaving little time to devote to you, this issue will manifest in the relationships you are most highly drawn to.

Rebecca is from a stable family, but her father's career escalated when she was very young. As a result, he spent a great deal of time away from home and she never had the opportunity to get close to him.

*I recently broke up with my long term boyfriend who is a wonderful guy but I was not in love with him. There was no chemistry or attraction but we had very good communication and conversation. I could not even stand the thought of kissing him.*

*I do still feel some guilt for leaving someone who was wonderful to me. I feel guilt for having hurt someone who did not deserve it. I have started seeing someone else and have been dating for about five months. Carl is a wonderful Christian but very different from anyone I have ever dated. He is a little more reserved in the way that he pursues me. I have always had guys be very persistent and forward with their feelings for me.*

*He tells me he is crazy about me but doesn't feel comfortable showing his feelings because I don't open up and tell him my feelings. We do not communicate well. We care for each other but it is obvious that neither one of us is completely secure or comfortable in the relationship.*

*The things that were missing from my other relationship are very strong in this one and vice versa. I am very attracted to him and can't wait to see him and spend time with him but sometimes I feel like I am going from one extreme to the other.*

*I don't know if I am being dramatic and this is just how things can be at the beginning of a relationship or not. I just know that I don't want to waste any more time trying to make a relationship work that I shouldn't. Am I being overly cautious?*

In her heart, Rebecca fears vulnerability, which explains why she chose to have a long term relationship with someone who treated her like a queen (to make up for the lack of attention she failed to receive as a child).

He fulfilled the fantasy she longed for from her father. However, since she had not worked through this issue, she kept her emotional armor in place and did not allow herself to be completely vulnerable with her boyfriend.

Rebecca will have the highest chemistry with men who ignite the feelings she had as a child with her father. That is the reason she attracted Carl into her life: to work through her issue of emotional abandonment.

## No One Will Love You as Much as I Do

Our core beliefs are so strong and controlling that we instinctively set the stage so we can recreate the powerful feelings we have not resolved from our childhood sorrow. Isabel is dealing with the realization that her boyfriend has deeply betrayed her.

*I am a 26 years old female student in graduate school and I've been in a relationship with a guy for more than two years. He is twenty years older than me and we are living together.*

*He had a previous marriage and two kids (21 and 18 years old). He has lost his oldest son in a car accident four years ago and this has caused a lot of emotional pressure. After the accident he got divorced. We met and moved in together and I believed everything was great.*

*We had the best relationship any one could imagine. We enjoyed every moment together. He is such a nice guy who had a lot of passion for me. He told me every day how much he loves me and cares for me.*

*Now after more than two years, I noticed a significant change in his temper. He is moody all the time. Whenever I ask him about it, he gets so mad. He tries to avoid me. We don't have any communication. It has been so hard for me.*

*Finally, I discovered that he has found a girl on the internet and they send e-mails to each other daily. They started calling each other and that is how I noticed something was going on. I confronted him about the calls and asked him to be truthful.*

*He lied and lied and covered up his lies. Finally, he broke up with that girl but is still looking for another one to substitute her. I noticed that he asks any girl that sends him an e-mail (even for work) whether she is interested for relationship. I feel so bad for him.*

*I am here ready to give my love and attention and I am doing that because I love him so much. But he is looking for someone else. I love him so much and I cannot move on so easily. I want him back. I want our relationship to be like it was in the beginning. I want everything to go back to that passionate loving relationship. What do you suggest me to do? What do you think I need to do? What should I do if he does not want to change?*

Isabel attracted a man who is obviously not emotionally free for commitment. She does not realize that what he is doing is not a reflection of anything she did or did not do in the relationship. Her boyfriend had been through two traumatizing events in a short period of time and should not be seriously involved with anyone during this time, as he does not have the capacity to be available emotionally.

Why did a young graduate student attract an older man noticeably not ready for a serious relationship? We learn the reasons by looking into Isabel's past. Growing up, her mother was psychologically unstable, experiencing a chronic case of post-partum depression. She completely withdrew from Isabel.

Because this happened on a regular basis, Isabel grew up believing that she was the cause of her mother's moodiness. Her mother was physically there, but the manner in which she related to Isabel was unpredictable.

Isabel needs to find the courage to end this relationship before more time passes. Her current boyfriend is in a totally different life stage than she is and more than likely would not want to start another family or remarry.

It is important that Isabel work through her issue of abandonment before getting involved with someone new. If she does not define her goals and become cognizant of the tendency she has to draw ambivalent men into her life, she will repeat this pattern.

## Once a Cheater …

Another manifestation of abandonment is becoming involved with a married man or woman. This is the ultimate in selecting a partner who is not obtainable on any level for a relationship.

Lily has unresolved feelings from her past and continues to attract men who are completely inaccessible. Unconsciously, she finds that they are safe because of their unavailability.

> *I am currently involved with a married man and would like to end the relationship but don't have enough power to do it. I recently ended a three year relationship because my boyfriend started talking marriage – which I'm not ready for. Now is seems that I can't detach myself emotionally from this married man.*
>
> *I met Thomas in class – he was one of my professors and the attraction was immediate. We first became involved while he was married to his first wife. He has now been remarried and seems to be unhappy.*

*When I graduated, he pursued me by telephone for six months. I finally gave in after breaking off my other relationship. The sexual encounter we had was great and now it seems that I want this man more and more.*

*Can you offer some advice? I just graduated from college and am off to a good start in my career but can't seem to make the right connection with an unattached male.*

Even though Lily has strong feelings for this man, he will cheat on her too if they end up as a couple. No matter whom he is married to, he will cheat on his spouse, believing he is unhappy.

His past actions are a clear indication of his present and future behavior. The key for Lily is to believe that she deserves to experience a devoted, affectionate, and caring partnership.

She must place a high value on herself and the love she brings to any union. One should never give such a special gift to someone who cannot reciprocate.

Lily grew up trying to get the attention of her father, who remarried when she was eight years old. Prior to her parents' divorce, Lily was her father's favorite child and enjoyed the attention he lavished on her.

After her parents divorced and he remarried, Lily's father distanced himself from his first family. Lily could not understand what she'd done to make her father leave. She felt totally abandoned.

As an adult she manifests this feeling over and over in her intimate relationships by selecting men who are not emotionally or legally available to her for true love. She recreates the feeling of abandonment through these relationships.

## Separated Is Just Like Divorced—Isn't It?

Another trap that recreates abandonment is getting involved with a man or woman who is separated. These individuals are not available, as they are still married, even if they are living apart from their spouses. As Melissa discovered, a commitment with a person who is emotionally unavailable falls apart quickly as soon as vulnerability matters arise.

*I am currently involved in a relationship that lasted five months with a man who was dating my girlfriend prior to dating me. My girlfriend was very upset with me and we have broken our friendship since then. She is spreading a lot of hurtful rumors about my past. I have told her secrets that I did not think she was going to divulge.*

*Anyhow, the man I was seeing has been separated for a year after a lengthy marriage. I have fallen deeply in love with him and don't want to let him go. He has broken up with me and has decided that he doesn't want to get involved at this time with anyone. I am very hurt as I thought he was falling in love the same way. I need to move on but feel very alone in doing so.*

*I don't seem to have the strength to accept that he has abandoned me. I am so tempted to call him but have to fight the urge every time. I don't want to be rejected anymore. Can you please offer some advice?*

Melissa's core belief of abandonment has spread not only to her intimate life, but also into her friendships. She believes that the root cause of her cycle of unsuccessful relationships is timing. Her low self-esteem and feeling of unworthiness also contribute to this recurring theme.

Childhood environments that are too secure and overprotected create abandonment problems in adult relationships based upon dependence. Further discussions with Melissa revealed that she believes she cannot survive alone; thus, she allows herself to fall into affairs that create a feeling of not being able to live without that person.

When it ends, she becomes nonfunctional in her day-to-day responsibilities. She does not tolerate loneliness for long and replaces the lost love with another strong person, whether friend or lover, to direct her through everyday life. As seen with the situation above, once the friendship with her girlfriend ended, she quickly befriended the boy-friend, with the unconscious agenda to replace that strong figure in her life.

## Our Relationship Must Fulfill My Needs

A cycle that recreates childhood abandonment due to unresolved feelings toward a parent is evident in the relationship between Mark and Suzanne. Both were emotionally abandoned as children—Suzanne by her father and Mark by his mother. Because neither resolved those feelings toward their parents, they recreated their childhood traumas as adults. Both believed the other had problems to resolve before committing to marriage.

> *For the past year, I have been dating Suzanne. She has dated a number of people before we became involved, including two individuals, Doug and Sam, as have I with other women prior to meeting her.*

*Suzanne dated Doug for approximately two years, and became engaged to be married. He disappeared, inexplicably, for about a month and thereafter the engagement was called off. They had power struggles over living arrangements and money. Anyway, the relationship ended, or so I thought.*

*I was initially attracted to Suzanne because of her commitment to Christ, her fun nature, good heart, sense of humor and attractiveness. We clicked wonderfully.*

*Doug and Suzanne continued to talk well after their break-up and continued to talk well into our relationship, until (I thought) it became an issue between us. I told Suzanne that I didn't feel it was appropriate for her to continue talking to her former fiancé, while she was forming a deep, loving relationship with me.*

*I believed it interfered with her efforts to bond with me. So, she told me that they agreed not to call each other but would send an occasional e-mail from time to time. I routinely, thereafter, asked whether there had been any continued contact and was routinely told that "No, I haven't talked to him."*

*Later in the year, I specifically asked whether she had heard from Doug and was told, "I haven't thought about him in months - he isn't even a blip in my think-*

*ing." It turns out she had been on the phone with him for that very day.*

*In the following year the extent of their continued contact came to light and I confronted Suzanne about it. She had repeatedly lied to me.*

*Her response was initially to deny it, but then she confessed that yes, they had continued contact, that they were just friends, that Doug was engaged and that there was nothing to fear about their continued contact. She denied that she ever told me that they would stop telephone contact and maintained her position, at least with me publicly, that she hadn't done anything inappropriate. She did admit that lying about this issue was inexcusable and that she would NEVER lie to me again.*

*Needless to say this has caused SUBSTANTIAL friction. I was prepared to ask Suzanne to marry me until all this and now I am in total limbo.*

*Her lying to me was a complete lack of respect and care for my well-being. As Christ has taught me, I can forgive for that if I am assured that the lying is not continuing. That doesn't mean I'll forget, but in time, I can forgive.*

*Am I off base, there? Second, am I overreacting to this continued contact with Doug?*

*I love Suzanne very much and my family loves her too - but I have been crushed by these revelations.*

*I think Suzanne is afraid to give Doug up for fear about some sense of vulnerability or loss of control. There is some deeper psychological issue here, which is really feeding this, but I don't know what it is.*

During her childhood, Suzanne's father was an upper-management executive. His position required that he move often and uproot the whole family. When Suzanne was in early adolescence, her family left an area where she had many friends and moved to a suburb where she knew few people.

She made few friends, other than one girl who had a borderline personality disorder. This friendship was a very destructive one in which Suzanne became involved in this girl's behavior with drugs, men, etc. This girl manipulated and used Suzanne, and to this day, she swears off any talk of high school.

Her feeling of emotional abandonment from her father led her to attract destructive relationships early in adolescence. Her feelings of abandonment escalated when her father chose to focus his energy on Suzanne's mom and older sister. She was left to be influenced by her friend and led down an unstable path.

After a painful breakup, she resolved to never let herself get to the point of being "dependent" on anyone the way she was with her former boyfriend. However, she is very dependent on everyone around her to help her take on her daily tasks. Her reliance on her parents is substantial. In order to keep her fear of vulnerability hidden from others, Suzanne is a control freak. She does not want anyone telling her what she can and cannot do.

Suzanne's abandonment issue is based upon dependence, even though she creates the façade that she is completely independent.

We tend to attract partners who bring about situations that place us in emotionally uncomfortable situations. We do this without thinking to force ourselves to deal with the feelings we have hidden and pretended to be resolved.

When we go back even further, we find that Mark's feeling of abandonment started with his relationship with his mother. She is an alcoholic, who became self-absorbed and manipulative early in his childhood.

Mark and his siblings have been codependents for their mother, nurturing her physical and emotional needs to try to keep things in balance. We see even more self-destructive cycles replay as Mark explains further.

> *I was an adult before my time and my mother was emotionally unavailable. When her alcoholism set in, the arguments with my father became more frequent as did her emotional outbursts and withdrawal to her room. As children, we thought we were the cause of her behavior. She eventually had an affair which led to the destruction of my parents' marriage.*
>
> *Despite her actions, I have loved my mother deeply. However, I along with other family members have always assumed responsibility for my mother's actions. To this day, she uses her love as a tool of manipulation.*

*I cannot forgive my mother because she will not acknowledge her behavior or take any responsibility for her actions.*

The core of Mark's abandonment problem starts with his feelings towards his mother. To this day he does not feel that she has taken responsibility for her actions and has not expressed any remorse for her behavior toward him, especially during his formative years.

Because he has not forgiven his mother for her behavior, he continues to attract women who create a similar situation. Instinctively he is comfortable with the tension that his core belief creates. His lack of forgiveness and his need to hear his mother's regret for what happened only hurt his chances of living a secure life in a mutually loving and esteemed relationship.

If we were to take this even further back, we would find that Mark's mother is an adult child of an alcoholic and experienced basically the same type of emotional abandonment from her mother. The cycle has repeated generation after generation.

Mark is the closest to drawing the line in the sand and stopping behavior from continuing. He is aware that he draws dysfunctional situations and is on the road to making the connection between his present circumstance and discord with Suzanne to his unresolved childhood feelings towards his mother.

## Is It Cold Feet, Or Does He Really Love Me?

Placing yourself in the path of a temptation as Jodie has done raises serious moral consequences. She unconsciously does not want to have a relationship in the true sense, so she seeks out men who are emotionally unavailable - such as Kevin. She is physically attracted to him, primarily because he is unavailable and is engaged to be married in a matter of weeks. As we saw with Lily, Jodie finds these men appealing because she is afraid of being vulnerable in her relationships.

*I feel ashamed of myself because I hung out with this guy from my grad school class. He is very attractive and athletic and we have an obvious connection. He was trying to set me up with his room-mate, or so he said, so he would call of-ten. But when I hung out with him on Friday night, he admitted to having all sorts of feelings for me.*

*Kissing and a few other things did end up happening, but the worst part is he is get-ting married in three weeks and the en-tire reason why I never wanted to hang out with him in the first place was be-cause I was sexually attracted to him and I liked him and I knew he was engaged.*

*So I tried to keep my distance and play it cool. He said he was confused and he loved his fiancé, but then I walked into his life and things just changed. Is that even possible? It sounds like a movie or something.*

*The bottom line is I feel awful for what I did. I don't even know his fiancé but it's wrong, plain and simple. I have had feel-ings for him, but stayed away because obviously I have no chance. He is getting married for goodness sake!*

*I don't know what to do. If he calls the wedding off and wants to be with me, how do I know he won't do the same thing to me? Should he call his own wedding off? I am very upset about my-*

*self and the situation I allowed to hap-*
*pen, so please help me.*

Jodie is attracted to the drama of the moment – she asks herself, "Will he leave his fiancé for me? If he does will he cheat on me in the future? Am I so captivating that Kevin will leave his life behind and pursue me?"

Morally she admonishes her behavior, but secretly relishes the adrenaline rush from the creating chaos in several lives. She wants to be rescued in her relationships, like she wanted her father to do when she was a child.

Jodie's father suffered tremendous financial setbacks during her preteen years and withdrew from her because he felt he let the family down. Because he felt like a failure as the provider for the family, he chose to isolate himself from his wife and children.

Eventually, the financial stress led to her parents divorce and her father's slip into depression. The consequences of adding physical loss to the emotional abandonment in her day to day life allowed Jodie to form a core belief that the men Jodie loves will eventually leave her.

To this day, Jodie tries in vain to get her father's approval, attention and love. Because her efforts are not reciprocated, she creates the feeling of abandonment in her intimate relationships and attracts men who are totally unavailable.

## *Defining Abandonment*

Our relationship with our parents is an important building block for our adult partnerships and personality, and serves as the model for what we believe intimacy should be like. That union becomes what we view as normal, and as adults we attract individuals who create that dynamic in our relationships. The ties we have to our mothers in particular are the basis of our adult personalities. When our mothers nurture us, we develop a feeling of security that gives us a positive self image and allows us to explore our surrounding world. If we do not receive this nurturing, we become insecure. This first emotional bond forms the basis for all our subsequent relationships.

The origins of your abandonment issues may include one or more of the following:

- Your mother was separated from you for a long period of time.
- You were raised by nannies or sent to a boarding school at a young age.
- Your mother was emotionally unstable.
- Your parents divorced when you were very young.
- You were overprotected and did not learn how to deal with life on your own.

The widespread abuse of alcohol leads many people to suffer through emotional abandonment because their parents who drank were self-absorbed in escaping themselves.

They did not have the capacity to nurture their children and provide the love and attention they needed in their formative years. As adult children of alcoholics mature, they attract individuals and/or situations that create the chaos they are comfortable living with.

## Drama Makes Me Feel Alive

Do you attract partners who are "drama-holics"? Gwen is engaged to a man who pretends to leave her whenever he gets upset at her. She writes:

> *What can I do about my fiancé? Every time he gets mad at me he threatens to leave. He even goes so far as to pack up his clothes and takes them out to his car. Sometimes he'll actually leave for thirty minutes or sometimes he just sits outside*

*for a little bit. He then comes back and says he doesn't want to leave and tells me that I make him so happy. He says he just doesn't know what to do when he gets mad.*

*Most of the time I don't even know what he's mad about. The last time he did it I told him that he can't keep doing this to me. I told him that if he did it again I wanted him to just go and not come back. I said I couldn't take not knowing if this is going to be the time that he really leaves.*

*He also has a very low opinion of women in general. He has said that women are liars, cheats, whores, and he can't trust any of them. I've tried to convince him that not all women are like that.*

*He tells me one day that I am the best thing that's ever happened to him and a couple of days later he'll get mad about something and I'm "just like all of them."*

*I don't know if I can take this emotional roller coaster ride much longer. When he asks why I always give him a second chance, I tell him that I will fight for any-thing as long as I think it's worth fighting for.*

*Most of the time I think this guy is worth the fight, but how do I convince him that I deserve to be treated better? I am a good-hearted woman that doesn't want to*

*hurt anyone, but how much hurt do I*
*have to take before he realizes this?*

Gwen grew up in a family where her parents abused alcohol. Her role in the family was that of peacekeeper. Her parents fought so much that she constantly felt as if she lived in a war zone. She believed she was in charge of keeping the family together, which caused much anxiety and fear throughout her childhood. There was always a crisis in her house.

As a result, she unconsciously attracted her fiancé, George. The dynamic of their relationship creates the feelings of tension that they are both familiar with from childhood. They feel alive by this exchange of intensity, and it makes them feel reassured.

## I Deserve Better, Don't I?

Carla's abandonment issue manifested at an early age when she was put in the position of caretaker of her younger brothers. Her mother was an alcoholic and too inebriated to adequately take care of her children, so she relied on Carla, expecting her to act like an adult even when she was a child.

Carla filled the emotional void she felt from her mother's abandonment by busying herself with the care of her brothers. She is most comfortable when she is taking care of the needs of those around her. She suffers from low self-esteem, so she does not feel worthy of love deep down, yet she longs for marriage.

*I have been with the same man for almost*
*seven years and he finally proposed to*
*me on Christmas Eve. I started talking*
*about a summer wedding only to be shot*
*down. He said we should wait until the*
*following summer so that we could get*
*some things done around the house. Well,*
*the summer is here with no wedding*
*plans in sight. There is still work to be*

*done around the house and he'll probably just keep using that excuse. As a matter of fact, he has ignored me when I start talking about wedding plans and will not sit down with me to set a date. His brother proposed to his girlfriend last October and is set to be married this October. His sister just met a man not even a year ago and already they are getting married next summer. I am very happy for them but also a little hurt inside.*

*We have lived together for five years and I know that he loves me. His family tells me that he's always been like this with all of his relationships. I guess I am afraid that I am not good enough for him. We have a great relationship, and of course we have our ups and downs but he seems to blame me for everything. I know that I am not perfect, but he is never wrong and that tends to make me a little afraid to approach him with matters I want to discuss.*

*I am afraid if I lay down the law and say I want to get married next summer, or else, he'll say there's the door. He has made comments to me like, "I would marry you but you have changed." I'm going to be honest with you: I am putting myself through nursing school right now with a goal of obtaining a Master's Degree. I work full time, go to school, keep an immaculate home, and make sure there is dinner on the table every night. I even make his lunches every night so that he does not have to wake up extra early.*

*I sometimes think he likes to make me feel insufficient or like I am hard to live with to get out of getting married. I am being honest: he is the one that is very hard to live with.*

*I don't want to leave. He is the love of my life. But my heart keeps getting walked on and I keep getting told negative things about myself. As a matter of fact, our sex life is very minimal. He even told me that if I get in shape he will give me more sex. (I am 5'5" and weigh 130. I don't see my-self as overweight.)*

*Without being conceited, I am a very pretty girl. I get attention from men all of the time. Again, I am not conceited, but do notice other men looking at me. I ac-tually hate going to public events with him at times because he is horribly jeal-ous and we end up arguing because he sees men looking at me. However, he can look until his eyes jump out of his head.*

*I am really frustrated. He doesn't treat me really bad or anything. He is home every night with me and overall, we have a pretty good relationship. I tell myself not to complain because other people have it a lot worse than I do.*

*But my heart is feeling so much pain and confusion right now. Am I wasting my*

*time? I know I don't need him because I
can support myself. But I need him emotionally. Or do I?*

Upon further discussion, Carla revealed that her boyfriend also grew up
in the family of an alcoholic. Marriage will not resolve his demanding
need for perfection from her, belittling and disrespecting her.

She is fearful of leaving this man, but she is facing life-changing
decisions at this point. Carla wants to have children and her boyfriend
is ambivalent about the topic. This was the turning point for Carla to
have the courage to leave her boyfriend and deal with her abandonment
issues. She wanted to break the cycle of emotional and verbal abuse
and knew she could not do that in a relationship with someone who
could not acknowledge the crisis.

## *Where Do I Go from Here?*

You can change your situations, but first you must investigate your past and see what childhood incidences contributed to and formed this core belief. The best place to start is by reviewing your current reactions to situations that bring up this feeling of abandonment and remember when you felt that way as a child. Intentionally becoming aware of the events leading up your adult beliefs will help you change your reactions and overreactions to present-day events. You will then be able to recognize the triggers that bring about your response.

In order to recognize the triggers that set your abandonment schema in motion, I encourage you to keep a journal of your primary relation-ships. Keep an account of the times you feel yourself reverting back to the fear you had as a child and what was happening at that time. Keep in mind that your schema can show up not only in romantic relation-ships, but also with people at work, school, family members and friendships.

The more pronounced your schemas is, the more likely you will begin to see how it manifests in many areas. Do not panic if you see a pattern of behavior emerge in your interactions with others. On the contrary, this revelation is the start of the journey.

Our greatest gifts are found by facing our fears. Facing your childhood worries of abandonment as an adult and bringing the truth to light will set you emotionally free of the cycle you have unconsciously subjected yourself to as an adult.

Look back at your last three significant relationships:

- Do you see similarities in each case?
- Were these relationships unstable and inconsistent?

If you grew up with instability in your childhood that you have not dealt with, you will be most attracted to individuals who generate feelings of instability. It is important to be knowingly aware of this tendency so you can avoid forming relationships with people who trigger this response.

When a stable person enters your life, trust that this person will not leave you. Give this feeling of stability the time and energy necessary to form a foundation of mutual trust and friendship before diving into intimacy.

# Chapter Three
## How Can I Trust You with My Heart?

### Unraveling the Pain of Childhood Mistrust and Abuse

In dating situations and/or committed relationships, are you attracted to people who are out of control?

Have you been involved with people who are have anger issues, have problems maintaining their temper, and take excessive opportunities to humiliate and criticize you?

Have your former dating partners exploited your weaknesses, cheated on you, disrespected and manipulated you?

If you expect others will hurt, abuse, or take advantage of you by cheating, lying, manipulating, humiliating, or physically harming you, a fear of mistrust and abuse controls your behavior.

### I Just Want to Be Loved

Carol is married to an emotional abuser. Ron uses his temper to maintain control over her and their children. He does not trust anyone, even his wife. As a young child, Ron was physically abused by his father. Although he does not hit his wife and children, the emotional abuse is debilitating on the family. Ron has not learned to be in command of his anger and takes out his feelings of frustration on those closest to him.

*I have a confused mind right now and don't quite know where to go. I have been working with this guy at work for about six months now and I am not sure how I feel. He makes me smile and laugh and I haven't done that in months now.*

*I have been married for fourteen years and not sure on if I'm happy at all. If I laugh and have fun with the kids my husband tells us to shut up. It's like prison at home. I have never told any one this because I am ashamed of my unhappiness.*

*My husband now wants me to quit my job of five years and stay at home with the kids. I feel he wants to keep me down as much as he can. I was very depressed before I went to work. At least there I can laugh and smile. My job is in management so I'm not at a low paying job.*

*I have never cheated on my husband, but I sometimes have thought about it, mainly here lately with this guy at work. I just want to be held and loved. Every day I go home my husband does nothing but complain and wonder what I can do for him.*

*My husband also doesn't want anything to do with the kids. He screams and yells at them too. I have been raised to stay with your husband, but I'm at my wits end with this. I only have one life and this one isn't what I want. Should I try and hold on to this relationship or what?? There is no physical abuse.*

50

In order to cope with the abuse he suffered, Ron learned to dissociate whenever he feels vulnerable. Carol feels unloved, unappreciated, and unwanted when Ron shuts down. Ron assumes that people secretly mean to harm him, so when Carol or his children do something nice for him, he automatically believes that there is an ulterior motive. He expects everyone will lie and take advantage of him.

Carol is vulnerable to her coworker and on the verge of an emotional affair because her marriage represents feelings of anger or the silence of being tuned out. She is desperately hungry for love and connection.

If you see yourself in a similar circumstance, you hide behind a wall of mistrust to protect yourself and never let people get too close. You are skeptical of the intentions of others and usually assume the worse. You expect betrayal in love. You avoid commitments altogether, form superficial unions, or select people who treat you badly and then feel angry and vengeful toward them.

Your childhood was unstable. You might have lived through emotional or physical mistreatment. Fighting in the family was not within normal boundaries. As a result, you had a strong feeling of not being protected as a child. As an adult, you are most attracted to individuals who are abusive in some way because it feels comfortable to you.

## My Relationship Radar is Broken

Here is Joyce's story:

> *I was the second child of four daughters and I had a very physically and mentally abusive step-father whose own father (my step-grandfather) molested me. I got married to a verbally abusive man at seventeen and divorced him six years later. I remarried again when I was 28, this time to a very sweet, adoring, nice man who turned out to be a child moles-*

51

*ter. He molested my older two daughters, after I'd had two more daughters with him.*

*My third relationship was with an extremely closed man. Our intimate relationship was great but the rest of the time he kept to himself leaving me to raise my kids and his daughter, and deal with everything else. After three years, I decided that I wanted to have a better relationship with someone I felt really loved me, not someone who just wanted a maid to sleep with. So, I took a break from relationships for a few years and just dated and worked on myself.*

*I moved away and met a man who lived in another town about 200 miles away and we hit it off. We saw each other every other week for a couple of months, but then my busy time of the year started. We knew our time would become scarcer, but he promised that we would find a way to talk every day, and even meet halfway for a few hours just to see each other.*

*As time went on, he became less available and I became needier because I didn't want the relationship to end. I'd fallen in love with him, and he said he loved me too, even though he wasn't crazy about having a long distance relationship. As I felt him pull away, I realized that I was spending more time feeling insecure and bad about our relationship than I was feeling good about it.*

*I told him that it would be better if we just remained friends and dropped the "relationship" part, because it was obvious to me that he was not keeping his end of the bargain.*

*I felt that being single and having the type of job that he did, that he would make time for me. Even though I was a single mother and working over 40 hours each week, I was still sacrificing to make time for him. He didn't argue, try to win me over, promise to do better or anything, just said fine. That hurt because part of me wanted to believe that if he loved me, he wouldn't want to leave me, but apparently he didn't really love me. I don't know.*

*I feel as though my self-esteem is still low when it comes to men, even though I've spent years and years in therapy and self-help trying to get rid of my self-esteem issues. I also feel that my intuition is still out of whack about men.*

Emotional abuse is defined as rejecting, ignoring, criticizing, isolating, or terrorizing other people, all of which have the effect of eroding their self-esteem. Emotional abuse is usually experienced through verbal attacks leading to rejection or belittlement. If your mother failed to instill in you a sense that she would take care of your basic needs, you will learn to mistrust others. Your first encounter with trust is vital to your overall core belief of having faith in others.

Abuse brings out feelings of pain, rage, and grief. The feeling of not being protected is a factor in most forms of abuse. One parent or caregiver may have abused you and the other did not prevent it or stop it. As an adult, you may experience volatile moods and easily become upset, which takes others by surprise in your sudden change of moods. At other times, you feel like life is unreal. You feel out of it. Abuse created strong feelings of defectiveness and makes you ashamed of yourself. You believe that you deserve abuse. You do not have a basic sense of security and so do not feel relaxed in relationships.

Even in a non-abusive situation, you may do things to make good people seem like abusers by twisting what they say, taking innocent remarks as insults, and magnifying their disloyalties while minimizing their acts of love. You can't accept when someone does something nice for you because you feel there must be an ulterior motive. You may also have a deep despair about life, low self-esteem, and feelings of defectiveness.

## Nothing's wrong with Him, So I'm Bored

Marissa wants to leave her emotionally and verbally abusive husband, but is torn because her heart says to leave and her mind tells her all the reasons she should stay. Adopted as an infant, Marissa first experienced verbal abuse from her adoptive father. Her attraction to her husband is the continuation of this cycle, which has been passed along from generation to generation.

> *I am having a very hard time leaving my marriage. I know it is bad, and I recently found out he was not faithful. He's not like a normal cheater though and thinks this is all a joke.*
>
> *He has been saying hurtful things to me as if I'm the one who did something wrong. I can't help but believe some of these awful things. In the past he has been abusive, so why do I still have re-grets about trying to leave?*

*I have been seeing this guy who is wonderful, but because "nothing is wrong with him" I feel bored and find myself thinking more about my ex-husband. There's so much more that goes into it, and I'm just having an awful time. I feel like he is trying to intentionally hurt me by telling me all these things he did when we were married and how he "truly" feels about me (which is all very bad) just because he knows I might be moving on. I just don't know what to do. I also think he might be bipolar. Why is this happening??*

Marissa is torn because this behavior is well-known to her, and the functional, adoring behavior in her new relationship is foreign to her. She is drawn to what she knows, so her mind is trying to rationalize her husband's behavior and convince her to give their marriage another shot. Because her husband has learned of a new man in Marissa's life, he has changed his tactics and is lavishing her with heartfelt conversations.

*My ex has moved on from this angry phase to writing me e-mails everyday telling me how great I am, etc. etc. He has shared all of these things with me that I have never known about him, vulnerable issues, and things he felt that I had no idea he felt that way. I don't understand how he could have not shared these things earlier, because it definitely would have helped our situation. Is he doing this just because there is another guy around?*

*We do have a daughter together and sometimes I want to work things out because I don't want to feel guilty for passing up a situation where he was ready to work on our relationship issues.*

*I really like this new guy that I am seeing. We had sex (I feel like I shouldn't have) and now I am completely am losing interest. I want to be happy and he gets along with my daughter GREAT, but I don't like that I am jumping from one relationship to another. I don't want to hurt this guy, and I don't think he should just wait for me.*

*How could my ex-husband be so conniving? Does he really want to "win me back" and then hurt me all over?*

If Marissa returns to her ex-husband, the chain of emotional and verbal abuse will resume. She is correct that his caring attitude is insincere and only a ploy to get her to come back. She can break this cycle with counseling. She will need to recognize and be aware of the danger signs in the future and the tendency to be highly attracted to men who will lead her down this abusive path again.

This core belief originates in childhood experiences of abuse, manipulation, humiliation, and betrayal, such as:

- Family members were untrustworthy.
- Someone in your family physically, emotionally, or sexually abused you as a child.
- You were taught by your parents not to trust people outside the family.
- Certain family members were against you.
- You were called hurtful names.

## I Can't Trust You

Jan's story is a case of how abuse continues from generation to generation until someone has the courage to break the cycle. Because Jan grew up in a home where she witnessed physical abuse, emotional abuse, and violence, her adult relationships have reflected that experience. Her feelings are intense and simmer near the surface. Because of this trauma early in life, her experience with love has been a painful journey. She has found that relationships are not places to relax and become vulnerable but are dangerous and unpredictable. She has a core belief that people will hurt her, betray her, and use her. She feels she must always stay on guard. It is hard for her to trust others, even the ones closest to her.

> *I treat everyone like I would like to be treated which some people take as a sign of personal weakness. I had a very nasty stepfather that I didn't like. He beat my Mother a lot and hospitalized her. He knocked her unconscious and raped her. Eventually, he shot and killed her. I couldn't abide by him touching me, but even he didn't know that. I didn't want him getting on Mom because I was bad.*

> *I am actually surprised when the people I love do something nice. I don't trust. Haven't had a lot of reasons to do so. I am not sure I'll ever trust anyone, other than my children. They are good to me. I really tried to give them the security I never had, and as much affection as I had to give; which was surprisingly, a lot. I was always there for them, and they trusted me implicitly. I also made no promises that I couldn't keep. It's important not to do that.*

*I have been married to Donny for almost twenty years. For the first four of those years, he was a physical and mental abuser. I didn't fight back, but I wouldn't stay down. I felt if I stayed down, the next time he'd start where he left off. Treating him civilly didn't work. I finally fought back, and broke his nose. It worked. I was amazed it did. The physical abuse is ongoing.*

*I try to praise him and encourage him. There is a nice guy in there, really. He just doesn't get it. Or, he does, but he can't give that little bit back. He buys presents, he has stuck up for me; he doesn't run me down in public; he just hasn't caught on to the fact I'm not going to hurt him, maybe?*

*I am not socially adept. I'm not a klutz at it, and I don't act goofy, I am just uncomfortable out in a crowd. I carry it off quite well, though.*

*Despite the abuse, I feel that I can make the relationship between my husband and I work. I just miss not having someone I can relax with and talk to. I am careful not to hurt him, either, because he has been told he was stupid and ugly and most of the rest of the bad things people say to kids.*

*I knew that the problems were there, but when I was younger, they didn't manifest as they are doing now. It seems that about the time you get comfortable with who you are, you do something that seems to be stupid, but you can't help it. It just pops up and you find yourself doing stuff that you wouldn't have even thought of earlier. I get anxious and obsess. I lose my cool and panic. I know better, but there it is. No wonder so many acquaintances think I'm nuts.*

Intellectually Jan knows that physical and emotional abuse is not what makes a functional, affectionate, and loving marriage, but it's familiar to her. Because of her mistreatment, she will find that she is most attracted to abusive partners. They generate the highest chemistry for her.

You may assume that people secretly mean to hurt you. Being abused brings about a state of hyper-vigilance. You are constantly on guard. The feeling of not being protected is part of most forms of abuse. Cruelty of all types—physical, sexual, and verbal—involves that same strange mixture of hurt and love.

## *Where Do I Go from Here?*

To break this chain of mistreatment, you need the help and support of a therapist to walk you through your past memories of abuse. In most cases overcoming the effects of childhood abuse is not easy and cannot be done without a professional.

A therapist will provide a safe environment for you to face your demons. In many ways you are living as if you were still that abused child.

Your therapist will help you visualize yourself as strong and powerful against the aggressor in your memories. You will learn how to stop accepting blame for what happened to you. No child deserves abuse in any way, shape, or form.

# Chapter Four
## I Never Receive Enough Love

### *Feel empty, lonely, and emotionally detached?*

If you believe no one cares for you or understands you, a feeling of emotional deprivation controls your behavior.

In dating situations:

- Are you attracted to people who rarely listen to you?
- Are you drawn to aloof, untouchable people?
- Do you feel that the more you give in love, the less you receive, and therefore you feel misunderstood?
- Do you sense that your need for love will never be met adequately by anyone?

If you suffer from this pattern, you are probably attracted to cold and selfish people. You may be distant and self-centered yourself, which leads to dissatisfying relationships. You feel cheated and alternate between being angry about it and feeling hurt and alone. Your anger drives others further away and ensures your continued deprivation. You feel empty, emotionally disconnected from others. You really do not know what love is or what it feels like.

The origin of this core belief lies in your relationship with your mother. You might have received a less-than-average amount of nurture as a child and were not soothed adequately. You might have felt unloved because your mother did not give you enough attention. This could have instilled a feeling of emotional detachment from your mother. As an adult, you compensate for your feelings of deprivation by becoming demanding and narcissistic. You may act as if you are entitled to get all your needs met.

## He Loves Me, So Where's the Affection?

Sandy has been committed to Matt for several years. She knew from the onset that Matt was unable to show affection toward her. In the back of her mind, she felt that time would lead Matt to let down his walls and be affectionate, but that has not happened. She is frustrated because this is not the type of intimate relationship she wants to experience long term.

*I am at the end of my rope of my relationship now going on three years. My boyfriend told that he was not affectionate when we met. I said I could handle that. We have been living together for nearly the whole time we've been involved. In the past year he won't kiss me, make love to me and basically treats me like furniture.*

*I know that just because he can't show affection doesn't mean that he doesn't love me. I'm trying to deal with this but there are so many other issues, family included. I have fun with him. We go places and have a lot of the same interests. But if I wanted a roommate, I would have advertised for one.*

*I am having a very hard time with this and he said all I do is give empty threats. I'm also in an emotional turmoil at my job. My boss is trying to come up with*

*any and every reason to have me fired,*
*waiting for me to make any mistakes.*

As Sandy has encountered, many times we have the highest chemistry with people who trigger vulnerabilities. The strong chemistry is based on primary beliefs that we formed early in life that come to the surface when those feelings of vulnerability are not resolved.

The chemistry is not rooted on positive qualities that will make the union last. Further conversations with Sandy revealed that her boyfriend, Matt, was emotionally deprived by his mother in childhood. Many times people who faced emotional deprivation will say that they had a normal childhood. However, when they portray past romances or parental relations, a feeling of disconnection emerges.

By exploring his former relationships and how he interacts with his mother, Matt can share his vulnerability with Sandy and work toward a solid foundation. It will be up to him to decide if he is willing to do the emotional work required to make this happen. Sandy will need to determine if she is willing to help Matt get to the other side of this fear or close this door if he is not willing to do the work to achieve an emotionally balanced relationship with her.

The origins of emotional deprivation lie in the maternal figure (usually the mother, but sometimes another adult woman such as grandmother or aunt), as she is the center of the child's world in the first years of life. That first bond becomes the prototype for those that follow. Most close relationships will resemble that initial experience. With emotional deprivation, the child receives a less-than-average amount of maternal nurturance.

For example, a mother may have been aloof and unaffectionate, did not hold her child enough or give the time and attention necessary to instill a sense of security.

Many times the mother just isn't in tune with the child's needs and can't connect. The child grows up without a sense of being loved and valued, and is not given enough guidance.

## If I Pretend Everything Is Okay, It Will Be

In love, you will be most highly attracted to partners who ignite your core belief that no one cares for or understands you. Jon attracted Tracy into his life for a year and a half. She broke up with him when her fear of vulnerability kicked in, but she still hands him enough emotional crumbs to keep him hopeful for reconciliation. Because Tracy's behavior is similar to Jon's unaffectionate mother's, he knew not to push too many sensitive buttons while they were together, fearing she would flee. By pretending that everything was okay, Jon only extended the inevitable consequence of her leaving him and finding someone else who would not place too many demands on her.

*The woman that I love very much broke up with me. She was a little distant emotionally from the beginning, but we had a powerful connection. Her hesitancy was due to her a recent break up with a controlling boyfriend prior to our relationship. She is independent and growing emotionally and spiritually. After a year and a half together, she broke up with me and quickly became involved with a new boyfriend.*

*Tammy is an amazingly wonderful woman. I know that she did not take the time to heal from her former boyfriend, which was the biggest obstacle in our relationship. She is not able to communicate her feelings, wants and needs. It was even painful for her to talk to me about what was on her mind. I could feel her holding things in and that was causing her pain. Pain that she might have thought came from me.*

*To this day, her former boyfriend tries to get back together with her. She gets frustrated about it but never wanted to discuss it, so I did not push. I figured she would open to me when she was ready. I believe she is trying to block the feelings she has for me. I don't know what to do to get her to come to me and see what we can have. I do believe that God gave her to me and wants me to love her no matter what. My heart will not let her go. My mind will not let her go. This is the first time in my life I can't let go of a love for a girlfriend. I dream of her, I can feel her and hear her during the day. I am constantly thinking about her and things to share with her and do for her. That is what tells me that I am supposed to stay in her life. I am not supposed to just walk away from her.*

*I wish I knew what God was trying to communicate to me. I don't really know. I ask for the guidance every night.*

*It hurts me when Tammy shuts me off because I can see and feel how wonderful we can be together. I want to build and unbreakable relationship with her.*

*Were do I go from here? I don't feel like dating another woman. I just want to be back with Tammy. Right now she tells me she can only give me friendship. I don't know the reasons why she broke up with me. She only said that she was not in love with me and can't give me what I need. We were best friends and shared spiritually together. We both like a lot of the same things and enjoy the same activities. We had so much in common.*

*She told a mutual friend that she knows I'm trying really hard and doing everything right, but she's still not in love with me. She also told this friend that she's planning on slowly erasing me from her life. However, she also said that she misses me and can't imagine life without me.*

*I need to know how to win her heart back. I have lost a lot of me and feel very empty and closed because I can't call her or see her when I need or want to. I am trying to hang in there with her as a friend and hoping that she will be in love with me again. But I see her and feel her trying to block it or hide behind this wall.*

Jon cannot find the strength to release this relationship because this is the first person who has ignited his primary belief to such an extreme degree. He is paralyzed by his obsession with Tammy and has distorted what God is trying to do in His life.

God brings people into our lives for emotional healing and to bring us closer to Him. His will never includes a situation where you are consumed by another person to the point of idolization and lose the ability to interact with Him.

## If You Love Me, I'll Run Away

Sometimes the combination of a life-changing event, such as a parent's divorce, magnifies a core belief to the point of being unable to maintain long-term relationships. Even before her parents' divorce, Darla had already felt the effects of her mother's lack of empathy and nurturance toward her. As an adult, she pushed away men who wanted to get closer to her. She is fearful of letting anyone get too intimate and getting hurt.

*I sometimes think I'm even too messed up for one person to give me advice. I think I have a fear of intimacy and/or of falling in love, for fear I'll get hurt.*

*Every single relationship I've been in, I've run away from, for fear that for whatever reason, I'll get rejected, I'll get hurt, or something bad will happen...or even something good. I tend not to give many men a chance. My last relationship was a little bit better in that I did give him a chance. I was with him for a whole five months.*

*Usually, my relationships end when I start avoiding my then boyfriend until it's a given that we're not together. The hint of a relationship starting is my cue to run. I don't feel I can trust anyone.*

*There's a relationship that I'm beginning to get into. We're still friends right now, but I know that he likes me, and I like him, yet I find my alarms going off and I'm avoiding him already. He wanted me to go to this wedding this weekend that*

*would have been over night and to a bar-
becue. I made an excuse that a couple of
my friends and my brother were coming
down and I wouldn't be available, which
was a complete and total lie.*

*I just was afraid of what might happen if
I went there. I'm tired of being afraid. I
want to give guys a chance and give everything that I'm afraid of a chance. Am I
hopeless?*

Every fiber in Darla's being tells her not to allow herself to be vulnerable with the people in her life. Her mind has formed a fundamental
belief that something bad might happen if she does. She would rather
lose the chance of finding love with this man than to take that risk. The
emotional armor she used to protect herself from her mother's lack of
nurturance, especially after her parents' divorce, has turned against her
as an adult trying to form intimacy. It is the barrier to the connection
she wants to encounter.

As a child, Darla's mother blatantly favored her brother, and she
continues to do so, even to the present day. Her lack of support for
Sarah's dream to go to college, in spite of her immediate support of her
brother's desire to go to college was the final blow. Sarah cut the ties
from that moment.

*If ever I tried to talk to my Mom about it,
she would nearly always get mad about
it. Another thing, after my Dad moved
out, everything went downhill. My
brother and my Mom started to fight.
When he finished high school she told
him he could either get a job or move out.
He chose to move out and live with my
Dad. He then decided to go to college.*

*She didn't really like that, but yet she still helped him out. She bought him some of the necessities he would need to get started so he wouldn't have to worry about that for awhile. Then my Dad and step-mom moved to a town that was about a half hour or so away.*

*That year I graduated from high school and I wanted to apply for college. When I went to my Mom, she refused to help me apply. I ended up staying home from school for a year and worked for about eight months. We started fighting about everything, so I moved in with my Dad. She was unhappy but eventually came to terms with it.*

*When I told her I was going to college she got really upset. She wouldn't help me at all. The school was two hours away and she only came to visit me once. The one time she did come to visit me, she only bought me junk and things I didn't need. I think I went to visit her Christmas weekend, and she did buy me some groceries.*

*She did more for my brother than she ever did for me, which I resent. If I ever tell her that, she gets mad and throws it back in my face. She'll twist it around and say she didn't visit or call me because I didn't visit or call her. I could go on about the things I've gone through and argued with my Mom but it would take ages.*

*Just remembering it again is making me upset. I don't like to remember these things. I know when I start talking to my Mother again, she's going to start crying, which makes me feel bad and it's not going to help much. Then I'll start crying and don't want to talk to her when that happens.*

Darla's issues today are a direct result of her mother's lack of nurturance, her parents' divorce, and a deep desire not to find herself in the same circumstance as her parents. Unconsciously, she pushes men away when she starts feeling vulnerable, fearing something that may or may not happen. It is her way of protecting herself emotionally. Even she realizes that's no way to live. She knows intellectually that her relationships do not necessarily have to turn out the same way her parents' marriage did, but she does not know how to get past the fear of allowing love into her life.

Darla's saving grace is the strong trust she has developed with her father and stepmother, who allow her to express her feelings freely and openly. With their strong support Darla gathered the strength and courage to face her mother and tell her how her actions made her feel in the past and how they continue to haunt her.

## *If He Loves Me, He'll Sense My Needs and Desires*

You may form a core belief early in life as a result of your emotional deprivation which dictates that people (especially relationship partners) should know how you feel without you telling them. You may reveal a little information and then have the expectation that others should know exactly where you are coming from without you giving the person the full picture. You then feel disappointed, hurt and angry when you are not understood. It is the starting point for your emotional deprivation cycle and sets the tone of the rest of the relationship/interaction. You eventually end up in the same emotional place after these old feelings are activated.

In your interaction with others, your emotional deprivation will be set into motion when you do not communicate your feelings and needs. When you recognize that this is an area that sets the process off, you must then become very cognizant of the need to clearly communicate your feelings, wishes and desires to others in order to avoid misunderstandings and most importantly, to avoid activating the cycle of the emotional deprivation.

In Kelly's situation, she has formed a core belief that true love means that her needs and desires will be met by her boyfriend without her expressing herself clearly. Since she felt betrayed by her mother and father when she was a very young girl, she uses this barometer to gage how her deep her connection is with the men in her life. Of course, this method has not worked well for Kelly, leaving her feeling lonely and disappointed in love.

*Kevin was my college sweetheart and I really liked him a lot. I always liked him, but we dated infrequently. We met again after college and he told me he really did like me but did not know how to express himself so he ended up ignoring me during that time.*

*We dated twice after college: the first time we dated he wanted to get married. I really liked him and wanted to marry him. I prayed about it. I felt if I did marry him he would ignore me and I would have a hard time with him loving me, as far as him spending time with me, and showing affection towards me.*

*I was afraid I'd be lonely in my relationship with him. I did not tell him this. I told him I thought our faith was too different, since he is Catholic and I am a*

*Christian. I told him he should look for a girl with a similar faith. Deep down I thought I would be lonely if I married him and I would have a hard time getting him to love me. So I broke up with him.*

*A few years late, I called him and we started talking again. We were both un-married and available. He asked me several weeks into our renewed relationship if I was serious about our relationship and if I wanted to give it a second try. I told him I was interested but we would have to work out the details since we lived in different states now. When I was flying to see him he told me he thought I was scared of him. Maybe I was because I knew he was always serious about marriage and I wanted to marry him too!*

*He called me a lot and was very loving and sweet to me. We went on vacation together for a week. I wondered when he would ask me to marry him. We did get in a small argument one afternoon during our vacation. He was moody and tired and wanted to pick a fight with me. I told him to stop.*

*I felt really uncomfortable with him flying home from the vacation. He was very quiet and would not speak to me. I did not feel good about this. When I got back home, he did not call me back. I did feel I received little in return in this relation-ship*

*I was very hurt and left him a message that he needed to call me so we could talk. I did not hear back from him. I emailed him earlier this year and prayed about what I should do about him.*

*I had a peace in my heart not to call him and that it was okay I did not marry him.*

One of the dangers in relationships is turning partners who initially may be a good match for you into another manifestation of your emotional deprivation. At the heart of Kelly's fear was her lack of trust towards those who loved her.

In Kelly's situation, she had an experience with her parents at a very young age which left her feeling devastated and betrayed. The incident left a lasting impression that if she told her parents anything private, they would broadcast her issues and problems to others. When her parents broke her confidence, she felt she could not confide in them or trust them from that point forward.

As an adult, Kelly tests her potential love interests by making them guess her what her feelings, desires and needs are in the relationship. Unconsciously she does this to prove her core belief that the people she loves are not to be trusted.

## Is He Just Into Sex - Or Do Little Gestures Mean Love?

Nicole senses that her relationship with Josh is one sided. What keeps her hopeful are the little gestures of affection he shows her every so often. She does not a strong sense of self to realize that her involvement with Josh is unhealthy and that he has a difficult allowing other people to love him. Josh believes no one really understands him.

*I have a situation that is very confusing to me. I was dating this guy, Josh for awhile and we were inseparable. When he went back to college, he went through depression and during this time we didn't talk. We didn't talk for about a month, so basically we broke up. He started to talk to me again and once in awhile we would see each other. Over the summer we saw more of each other and talked like we did when we were dating. During this time we started having sex. Well, we still talk and we still see each other almost every weekend.*

*My problem is that people say he's just using me for the sex, but the little things he does that confuses me. For example, one time Josh offered me a gesture that meant a lot to me. He always has to kiss me goodbye and has to make sure I get back home safely. It's not always sex when we're together - sometimes we'll just sleep side-by-side and that's the best time.*

*The other thing is that he'll talk to me for weeks then one week he'll decide not to talk to me. One time I was up in his area to visit a friend and he called me to help jump his car. He said there was no one else he could call?! I guess what I'm trying to ask is if he's just for the sex or is there more to it? Could he still have feelings for me?*

Josh's intense feeling of loneliness and disconnection with others led him to the verge of an emotional breakdown. He is not close to anyone, including friends and family.

Josh's mother became pregnant at an early age and he always sensed she wished she never had him. She was resentful that her friends were going out, having a good time – and she was "stuck" raising a child.

Josh never has felt close to his mother nor felt truly loved or understood by her. In his relationship with Nicole, he feels uncomfortable being in vulnerable situations with her and avoids emotional connection.

Although he longs for a relationship where he feels loved and understood, he unconsciously he recreates a feeling of disconnection in his intimate relationships, thus preventing the love he seeks from developing.

## Defining Emotional Deprivation

Emotional deprivation is difficult to describe. It is a rather vague sense that you are going to be lonely forever. It feels as if something is missing, as if your life is empty. In love you tend to be demanding, and there is an insatiable quality to your needs. No matter how much people give, it never feels like enough. You feel disappointed in others and let down in general. You received less-than-average maternal nurturing, and this absence led to your feeling of emotional deficiency.

As a child, how would you categorize your relationship with your mother?

- Did you feel close to her?
- Did she understand you?
- Did you feel loved and valued?
- Was she warm and affectionate?
- Did you love her?
- Could she give you what you needed?
- Could you tell her your feelings?
- Could you rely on her?

In romance, you may break off the relationship whenever your partner gets too intimate, or protect yourself from closeness by choosing partners who are unavailable. You might reinforce your deprivation by sabotaging it and becoming overly sensitive to signs of neglect. You can be demanding. You may not ask for what you want from your partner and then become hurt, withdrawn, or angry when your partner cannot read your mind and meet your emotional needs.

When we explored the issues facing Mark and Suzanne, we learned how Suzanne's abandonment fears affect their relationship. Mark has issues with emotional abandonment due to his mother's alcoholism, but his primary issue deals with the lack of nurturance he received from her as a child. She did not make him feel loved and valued, and he seeks that approval as an adult.

Looking at his primary relationships, it is clear that he is repeating a pattern and unconsciously playing out his unresolved feelings towards his mother. Because this core belief is so ingrained and has so scarred his soul, Mark is definitely in a spiritual battle. He is drawn to drama and chaos and truly feels alive when there is some type of upheaval going on. If everything is calm, he will create a crisis in order to get that adrenaline rush. He sets up elaborate, romantic, and expensive scenarios for his girlfriends. He unconsciously knows they will end in disappointment. He incessantly taps into this feeling of dejection. At the countdown to his wedding to Suzanne, an old girlfriend reappears in his life and complicates matters.

> *Suzanne and I are scheduled to get married next month. We postponed the wedding once to deal with some issues. We have been counseling with a pastor, which has gone well.*
>
> *The girl I dated very seriously for about eighteen months just before Suzanne contacted me out of the blue. Her name is*

*Elaine. Her father was abusive and an alcoholic.*

*I broke it off with Elaine after many promises weren't kept, and phone calls not returned. She would disappear and would make no significant effort to develop emotional intimacy with me. It was very much of a one way relationship. I gave and gave and gave and got very little in return.*

*All of a sudden, I get this rush of attention. Elaine tells me, "I love you. I made the biggest mistakes of my life, letting you go. I can't bear the thought of you with another woman. I have been going to intensive counseling and my issues are being worked out. I am setting boundaries and my work on that will be complete shortly. I want you back. When can we see each other? I love you."*

*Suzanne was aware of this onslaught and was there when some of the gifts Elaine sent me arrived.*

*I tell Elaine I am dating someone else and I am in love. This devastates her, but she doesn't give up. Letters, books, tapes, CDs, phone calls, packages in the mail. One day I walk out of a seminar and there is Elaine. She had called my office and they told her where I was and she showed up.*

*Then she calls me one day and tells me that her counselor was going to call me (her counselor had been calling me frequently, sometimes in response to my calls to her, because Elaine would make comments like she couldn't live without me, etc.), so I needed to stay at my office. Well, that was not true - she was two blocks away and wanted to surprise me. She had drawn this picture of us that is, admittedly, absolutely beautiful. I mean amazing. She said she had been working on it for months. I accepted it and she told me that she wanted to spend time with me and I told her that I didn't think that was possible. I haven't seen her since then and the phone calls stopped for a while. She would send me innocuous e-mail about her business or something and I would usually ignore those.*

*I called to check on her and to make sure she was alright. She didn't answer the calls and then I spoke to her briefly this week. She professes her love, and tells me that I am her soul mate and that she is mine although I won't say it.*

*She later explained that this occurred because she was going through intensive counseling at the time and didn't want to burden me with those issues until they were resolved and she wanted a second chance. I told her then that I was in love with another woman I told her I was engaged. She is upset that I didn't give her a second chance.*

*I am bothered by this and I believe that there is a reason I didn't give her a second chance. Suzanne is the first reason. The second reason is that I am wary of anyone who says they have changed so much that they can now include you in their life, when before they went to such efforts to keep you from knowing them intimately.*

*I know my first reason is valid. Is my second reason valid? I guess I have concluded that if my first reason is valid and the second doesn't matter. Elaine states she loves me with such incredible passion and vigor now that it really kind of frightens me a little from many different angles. I have told her and written to her that I don't think we should communicate. She has indicated that she will abide by that wish.*

*Why does this person have such a hold on me? I think it's not the person that has a hold on me but the feeling of guilt for being happy with someone else and the guilt for hurting someone else's dreams. Or is it because I yearn for this spontaneous affection?*

The last thought Mark has reveals what's in his heart. His ego rationalizes that he's inadvertently keeping Elaine from her dream of marrying him, but the truth is all about him.

He yearns for the kind of affection that Elaine is promising he can have with her. Because neither has worked through their respective problems, the relationship will play out the same as it did in the past. Elaine is especially attractive to Mark because she is the most passionate and dramatic of all his partners. A truly emotionally available person would hold no long-term appeal to Mark at this stage, as he would believe harmony was boring and lacked spark and attraction.

- In past relationships, did you drive away your partners with incessant demands?
- Did you get bored with someone who was treating you well?
- Did you not allow your partner to protect or guide you?

Sometimes coping with emotional deprivation leads to narcissistic tendencies. You might become demanding about superficial or material things, anything except what you really crave, which is emotional nurturance. As a result, you are never satisfied because the real need is not being met.

You may not have been allowed to be demanding about emotional needs as a child, but you were allowed to be insistent about other things. Because you do not acknowledge your emotional needs, your relationships are superficial and empty.

## *Where Do I Go from Here?*

It is important to become aware of your feelings of deprivation. Notice when you feel lonely, empty, or misunderstood in your current relationships with loved ones, family members, friends and work associates. When those feelings surface, work toward not rationalizing them away. Instead, analyze why you overreact to situations that do not warrant such strong responses. When strong feelings of deprivation surface, you know that your schema has been triggered. The connection can be found in your childhood deprivation and it is during these current episodes that you can pinpoint the pain you are unconsciously recreating.

The idea is to work your way back to the source of the feeling and reveal the first time you felt deprivation. As mentioned earlier, your feelings of deprivation can surface not only in your romantic relationships, but also in your friendships, work relationships, and/or academic relationships. Sometimes when the issue is particularly painful, you may experience degrees of your emotional deprivation in all the relationships you form. This is how unresolved pain is brought to the forefront so you may begin the process of healing.

If you choose to ignore these signs, you will find yourself in a cycle of similar relationship patterns. Each new person, particularly romantic will "seem" different but either you will mold the relationship in a manner that brings out your deprivation, or you will feel bored and unsatisfied because the intense passion is not immediately there.

So to change your emotional deprivation, it is vital to avoid cold, depriving partners, for they will generate the highest chemistry and trigger the cycle of bringing situations into your relationship that lead to these feelings.

When you meet someone who is emotionally available, give that person a chance and build a foundation of friendship and trust. Allow yourself to be vulnerable and share your wants, needs and desires with your partner.

Even though this type of relationship will not generate the kind of passion that you equate with love, resist the urge to leave because you feel unfulfilled. Do not let anger and resentment build up because you feel your wishes are not being met. You must learn to communicate your feelings and desires to your partner for a stable, loving, and lasting partnership to take shape.

You must take a leap of faith and allow yourself to be vulnerable so true and lasting love can be experienced.

# Chapter Five
## I Want Everything to Be the Best

### Why Monetary Gain and Career Advancement Does Not Guarantee Relationship Success

In dating situations:

- Are you attracted to the most beautiful and/or the most handsome person who is extremely talented and successful?
- Do you search of the perfect partner and unable to settle for less?
- Are you demanding and extremely critical with your partners?
- Do you expect your dates to live up to your standards?
- Are you attracted to perfectionists?

If you never can relax and enjoy life and always feel under pressure to get ahead, you allow your unrelenting standards to dictate your behavior. It is imperative that you have the finest house in the best neighborhood, the most luxurious and expensive car, a prestigious career, earn the most money, have the finest clothes and look the most stunning.

Your life is one big competition, whether you are working or participating in extracurricular activities. To you, your benchmarks appear normal so you take your accomplishments for granted. To others, you seem to have it all; a success at everything you do. The purpose of life for you is achievement. You do not allow yourself the chance to stop and enjoy yourself. Even when you are participating in sports or other recreational activities, you are competing and striving to outdo everyone else. You always feel there isn't enough time to do everything and may be constantly frustrated and irritated with yourself for not meeting all your criterions.

You believe that if you keep striving and pursuing perfection that you will attain it. You dream of reaching your goal of excellence and believe that when that moment comes you can unwind and enjoy life. However, that moment never arrives because you always find something else to pursue, which enforces your core belief. You feel very uncomfortable if you are not pushing yourself and reaching for the next performance level.

Unrelenting standards originates with your parents and your childhood was dominated by triumphs. Your parents may have been conditional with their love for you. They may have only given you affection, approval or attention when you were successful or perfect. When your parents display conditional love, your childhood is focused on winning their love. On the other hand, your parents may have smothered you with love and approval when you met their high expectations. To you, achievement was the ticket to winning their love. Because your unrelenting standards are learned from your parents, overly high expectations feel normal to you because it's all you have known. Others see your expectations as relentlessly high. Your parent's behavior and attitudes modeled their perfectionist, status oriented and overly excelling ways. As a child, your parents communicated their unrelenting standards to you either unconsciously or consciously.

## He Looks Like Marriage Material on Paper

Beth is a high achiever in her career but relationship success has eluded her. She longs for marriage and children and is frustrated that she cannot find a man who will commit to her.

> *My most significant relationship to date was with Edward. We met through a mutual friend who thought we'd make a good couple. Edward relentlessly pur-*

*sued a romantic relationship with me for months. I was not interested in dating him at first, but I did like his personality and enjoyed his company. We had so much in common. We both ran marathons and worked in the same field. He was very intelligent, had several advanced degrees and graduated with honors from a top Ivy League school.*

*I found his intelligence, career and education very attractive. He also had a wonderful family who welcomed me in to their circle. My parents are very particular about the men I date seriously, and they both loved Edward. All our friends thought we made a great couple.*

*After dating for a year, it was time to move our relationship to the next level – marriage. Edward shared my desire to marry and have children, but for some reason he decided not to marry me, which seemed out of character. I knew he was self-centered and selfish with his time and money, but I thought his priorities would change once we were married. I never found out why he couldn't commit to me when we fit together so well in so many areas.*

Beth mistakenly believes that credentials make the man. The men who date her must pass her internal check list before she will even consider a relationship. Beth came from a home where brilliance was required. Her mother expected Beth to do extremely well at everything she pursued. In exchange for her high performance she would shower Beth with love, attention and lavish gifts.

> *When I was a child, my mother pushed me to be the best at everything – good was not acceptable to her. She wanted me to be superior at everything. I believe her demands to get the very best out of me helped me achieve the success I enjoy today. I do think that her high standards have influenced who I select for my relationship partners.*

Because Beth's core belief that life is a series of achievements and rewards, she misses countless opportunities to develop a meaningful, fulfilling personal life. The very qualities and characteristics that Beth respects and attracts in a partner are the source of her discontent. The nature of these characteristics and the materialism she requires attracts self-centered and egotistical men.

Because she has primarily developed the masculine side of her personality to compete in her career, she has underscored her femininity. Power is important to Beth and she views the softer side of herself as a detriment instead of an asset to balance her personality.

Her competitive nature causes the men in her life to leave because they feel more competitive and combative with her. They do not believe she loves them for who they are, but what they represent. They do not believe she will love them and stay through tough times if they lost everything.

## *Defining Unrelenting Standards*

There are three types of unrelenting standards:

- Compulsive
- Achievement
- Status

## Compulsive

The compulsive person is someone who keeps everything perfectly in order. You are very detailed oriented and cannot stand to make mistakes. You cannot relax unless things are flawless, which they never are. You may blame yourself for your surroundings. You may focus on the one slight detail of a project or social occasion for example that did not go completely smoothly. You reproach yourself for not getting it right. Being compulsive is a coping mechanism you use to feel in command of your surroundings.

## Achievement

These are the workaholics. You place an enormous value on career achievement and getting ahead. You may be angry much of the time, whether your anger is directed at someone who has out performed you or internally for not living up to your capabilities. This type of unrelenting standard can be applied to any activity that should be a pleasure but you turn in to a chore and a means to compete.

## Status

If you have an excessive desire to gain recognition, status, material wealth, and looks then your unrelenting standard is status oriented. You have a sense of never living up to your expectations, no matter what. You beat yourself up and feel ashamed when you do not meet your goals. There is never enough money, power, status or looks for you to feel content. You feel driven to the next levels of success, as there is always someone with more than you. You may try to fill your emotional emptiness with secular success, which never works. You sit alone in your beautiful home surrounded by your state of the art technology and expansive art collection wondering why you feel so unhappy.

The main issue that people with unrelenting standards face is losing touch with their real self while building this façade personality. You are so blinded by achievement, status and orderliness that you do not develop the emotional and spiritual side of your personality. You do not have time for anything that does not promote your ideal self and pushes you higher. You do not value friendships unless there is something in it for you to advance your status.

## Where Do I Go From Here?

It is imperative that you make every effort to balance your life and learn how to alter your behavior in order to get your deeper emotional and spiritual needs met. Begin by examining areas where you constantly feel pressure to perform at a high level. List the advantages and disadvantages of meeting your standards. You probably benefit monetarily from many of your achievements, but the money has not brought joy to your life. You may see that the disadvantages destroy the quality of your life, as your relentless pursuit takes a toll on your health and emotions.

Once you see the benefits do not outweigh the disadvantages, you will be in a position to change your thinking about what makes life worthwhile. You need to decide what goals and achievements are important for your overall happiness and what goals you can let go. Perfection is not worth the emotional and physical demands they place on you.

## ·Part One Exercise·

### *Identifying Your Core Relationship Beliefs*

In order to recognize the self-defeating patterns and negative fundamental beliefs, I encourage you to describe your past three significant relationships and the feelings you associate with each one. By writing out what happened and the reasons why each ended, you will notice similarities. Through this identification, you can see what issues need to be addressed and resolved.

 In your past relationships, what core beliefs manifested?

Relationship One:

Relationship Two:

Relationship Three:

Noting the above core beliefs and relationship patterns that have emerged, the next step is to identify the origin of your fundamental relationship beliefs.

If any of the following statements are mostly to completely true of you, Abandonment is a very strong issue for you in your relationships:

- I worry that the people I love will die or leave me.
- I cling to people because I am afraid they will leave me.
- I do not have a stable base of support.
- I keep falling in love with people who cannot be there for me.

- People have always come and gone in my life.
- I get desperate when someone I love pulls away.
- I get so obsessed with the idea that my lovers will leave me that I drive them away.
- The people closest to me are unpredictable. One minute they are there for me and the next they are gone.
- I need other people too much.
- I believe I will be alone.

If any of the following statements are mostly to completely true of you, mistrust and abuse is a very strong issue for you in relationships:

- I expect people to hurt or use me.
- People close to me have abused me.
- Eventually the people I love will betray me.
- I have to be on guard from others.
- People will take advantage of me if I am not careful.
- I test others to see if they are really on my side.
- I try to hurt others before they hurt me.
- I don't allow others to get close to me because I expect they will hurt me.
- I am angry at what others have done to me.
- I have been physically, sexually or verbally abused by those I should have been able to trust.

If any of the following statements are mostly to completely true of you, Emotional Deprivation is a very strong issue for you in your relationships:

- I need more love than I get.
- No one really understands me.
- I am often attracted to cold people who can't meet my needs.
- I feel disconnected, even from those closest to me.
- I have not had one special person I love who cares deeply about what happens to me.
- No one is there to give me warmth, holding and affection.

- I do not have someone who really listens and is tuned into my true needs and feelings.
- It is hard for me to let people guide or protect me, even though it's what I desire.
- It is hard for me to allow people to love me.
- I am lonely much of the time.

If any of the following statements are mostly to completely true of you, Unrelenting Standards is a very strong issue for you in your relationships:

- I cannot accept second best and have to be the best at most of what I do.
- Nothing I do is quite good enough.
- I strive to keep everything in perfect order.
- I must look my best at all times.
- I have so much to accomplish that I have no time to relax.
- My personal relationships suffer because I push myself so hard.
- My health suffers because I put myself under so much pressure.
- I deserve strong criticism when I make a mistake.
- I am very competitive.
- Wealth and status are very important to me.

Once you have identified your fundamental beliefs, I encourage you to take your writing exercise a step further.

Reflect back on your childhood and write about where and when these emotions showed up in past situations. Go back as far as you can remember until you find the source and the cause.

I most identify with:

1) Abandonment because as a child the following experience happened:

It formed by core belief of:

2) Mistrust and Abuse because as a child the following experience happened:

It formed a core belief of:

3) Emotional Deprivation because as a child the following experience happened:

It formed a core belief of:

4) Unrelenting Standards because as a child the following experience happened:

It formed a core belief of:

# Part Two

# Heart Healing

In Part Two, Heart Healing you will learn how vital your spiritual maturity is to overcoming the emotional strongholds your schemas have placed on your relationships. Your total healing comes from not only intellectual knowledge, but through faithfully building your spiritual wisdom and placing your trust in God.

You will also read how to overcome negative, critical thoughts and the powerful steps you can incorporate to eliminate fear and live in control of your thoughts.

# Chapter Six
## The Power of Forgiveness

## *Goodbye Grudges, Hello Love: Forgiveness Heals*

Forgiveness is a gift you give to yourself. It is a release from past anger and pain and the burden of carrying resentment. When you resolve to forgive someone, you choose to live in the present. Forgiving does not mean forgetting, but releasing the damaging emotions and moving toward an emotionally stable life. Forgiveness does not mean you condone the actions of others.

The events you experienced have molded you into the person you are today; however, it is important not to let past pain and heartache define who you are. You do not want to carry your pain with you for so long that you become labeled by your suffering - such as the woman whose boyfriend cheated on her. Trials and tribulations are brought into your life to grow character, build your spiritual muscles, and most important, bring you closer to God. When someone wrongs you, God promises to give you double for your trouble if you have faith in His plan and will for your life.

It is up to you to decide not to be controlled by your circumstances and take the initiative to forgive those who do not know better. People tend to hurt others out of their own fear and pain. By forgiving those who hurt you and not holding a grudge, you are pleasing God. Your pardon will not go unnoticed or unrewarded.

Forgiveness allows love to enter your life. By clinging to anger, you permit your ego to relive the wrongs of your past. You allow your opinion of yourself to define you as a wounded person. Continuously reliving past anguish in your mind and verbally describing your situation to others gives life to your sorrow.

Most of us go through a period of mourning, especially after the end of a relationship, as we try to figure out what happened to the life we knew. It is natural to grieve a loss. The danger here is remaining in this phase and incorporating this stage into the essence of who we are. There are only two emotions: love and fear. By concentrating on fear—anxiety, sadness, anger, and pain—you block the very thing you want to attract, which is love. If you lead your life with your injuries, you cannot properly grieve, recover, and move ahead with life. It takes a conscious effort to let go of the temptation to be cynical, pessimistic, judgmental, and resentful about the end of a relationship or any other event or situation you feel is unforgivable. You may ask, *"Why should I forgive others when it was not my fault?"* There are five reasons:

1. If you do not forgive others, you cannot be forgiven.

2. Forgiveness is essential to your emotional healing. There is a vital connection between forgiveness and healing.

3. Forgiveness brings peace of mind. A guilty conscience cannot be at rest. Fear will take over your life and life will become torturous. All that is required is a prayer to God for forgiveness.

4. Forgiveness destroys your enemies.

5. Forgiveness can heal your broken family and bring it together again.

Through forgiveness, you are giving yourself permission to love yourself. You are acknowledging that you are worthy of love. You are designed to give and receive, not to hold on to anger, revenge, bitterness, and resentment. You open the door to physical illness, psychological damage, and soul despair by clinging to negativity.

There is no excuse for not forgiving. If you do not pardon others, God cannot forgive you. If God is perfect and He absolved you, why can't you, with all your faults, forgive someone else? How many people have you sent into an emotional jail because of past offenses that you will not forgive? God has forgiven you through the death of His Son, Jesus Christ. No defense or argument for your stance to avoid reconciliation is acceptable.

## I Forgive You, Until Next Time

Tony has trouble with the forgetting aspect of absolution. Some people say they have forgiven something in the past, but they keep reminding that person of what happened back then. That is not sincere forgiveness which must come from a pure heart. Saying the words but secretly holding on to resentment will not free you to live an emotionally abundant life.

> *I have been in my current relationship with my girlfriend for one year. I have a tendency to forgive her for things in the present (nothing serious), but dwell on them at a later time. This is absolutely the only problem we have in our relationship.*
>
> *I can sincerely understand where she is coming from and totally forgive her for something one minute, and then a week later it randomly pops into my mind. Then, I fixate on the issue that happened in the past and I have doubts of how much she loves me in the present.*
>
> *These bouts of stupidity never last for more than a few hours, but they are harmful to our relationship. I need tips*

*for forgiving in the long run, rather than
for a few weeks.*

Tony is consciously aware that his fixation on unresolved issues with his girlfriend is harmful to the longevity of their relationship. It erodes trust. Each time Tony revisits an issue in a confrontational manner, he chips away at the security of their relationship.

If he does not forgive and forget even mundane issues, he will drive his girlfriend out of his life. She will not feel free to express her emotions to him for fear of continued retaliation.

How does Tony get to that place of love, not only with his girlfriend, but with everyone in his life? Tony is guilty of judging others. You are judged by the same measuring stick you use to judge others. It is a wise and compassionate person who puts himself in the place of another and realizes the roles could easily be reversed.

When you suffer, either from others or from life situations that shake up your world, your human nature tells you to get angry and not to forgive what happened. You perceive a loss instead of a gain. But it is at these times that you stand to benefit the most if you can take the step of true forgiveness.

The power of forgiveness is great, but to truly release resentment takes a tremendous amount of courage and commitment. If your motivation stems from personal gain or a grudging belief that it is the right thing to do, you will not realize the true benefits of forgiveness.

A genuine value must be placed on forgiveness for the sake of the offender. If you forgive others, you operate from a position of strength, physically and mentally.

## Am I Sabotaging My New Relationship?

If you do not release built-up resentment and anger from a previous relationship, you will carry those feelings over into the next one, as Jeremy did.

*After being married for over 11 years and divorcing because we drifted apart, I found myself in a love relationship five months later. In the beginning, like most relationships, it was nothing but excitement. Just the thrill of talking to each other was more than any two months put together of my previous marriage.*

*We had a definite physical attraction from the get go, and as I got to know her, I really became interested. We had similar ways of thinking and of growing up, which made me feel like she understood me. Now after being together, living together and proposing to her it seems all I can do is look for the things in her that I don't enjoy. Things I'm sure existed before, but I didn't pay attention to. She is still the strong, beautiful, sexy, and caring person that I met, but I can't seem to stop thinking of all the things that I don't like.*

*Is this because of my fear of being hurt again, or is it that I've reached a point in the relationship that I am actually weighing out what matters most to me for a life partner? Either way it doesn't make me feel good because I do love her.*

Jeremy's fear of vulnerability emerges as his feelings evolve from physical attraction to an emotional attachment. His fear of being hurt again is magnified primarily because he has not taken the time to forgive what happened in his marriage. He is fearful of being vulnerable in another commitment that runs the risk of emotional pain. Without thinking, he will repeat the same pattern if he does not resolve the fundamental beliefs that led to the end of his marriage.

- Do you feel anger or rage and cannot understand why?
- Do you feel people will eventually hurt you?

Anger is a motivational force. It can be a driver for success or a leader to failure. Carrying pain, anger, previous hurts, rage, and grudges against others serves no purpose. It is completely consuming and affects how you relate to others. Deceiving yourself does not make the grief invisible. Others see the anger in your actions and hear it in your tone of voice. It is the wall between you and the love you seek.

Forgiveness is not one single action, feeling, or thought. It must become a way of life, renewed every day. How do you forgive those who have hurt you earlier and shed the sorrow, anger, and loneliness that hamper you today?

Where do you start in order to give yourself permission to heal?

Here are five steps I encourage you to take to release your resentment and anger.

## *Step One: Acknowledge Your Pain*

To truly forgive, the first step involves admitting what is bothering you and how it makes you feel. Suppressing your grief will not make it disappear. Until you go through this process, the pain will only resurface in future relationships.

One way to accomplish this step is to journal in detail any past actions you can't forgive yourself for and any wrongs done to you that you cannot release. Once you have finished, read the list and take comfort in the wisdom that you did the best you could with the information you had at the time.

Forgive yourself and free the anger and hurt around this person and situation. Liberty from a distressing event will be achieved when a discussion concerning what happened does not create anguish or agony in your heart.

Your sorrow is very real, so do not minimize it or try to bypass the mourning period. You must go through this grieving stage in order to release your pain.

## Step Two: Allow Yourself Time to Grieve

Facing heartache can be frightening, but by fully experiencing the sadness, you will keep it from dominating your life. Many people are taught to suppress their negative feelings toward others because those emotions are viewed as wrong. Being stoic will not free you from distress. Do not deny yourself the opportunity to grieve.

It is human nature to immediately seek to replace what we believe we have lost. I encourage you to view these times as opportunities to grow in your walk with God. He uses situations where you do not feel invincible and full of pride in yourself to communicate with you. His will is to have a close bond with you, not only during times of crisis and sadness, but each day of your life. By experiencing the full extent of your dejection, you will be able to see the good in what happened.

## Step Three: Examine Your Perceptions

Making sweeping judgments can keep you in a cycle of replicating dysfunctional patterns. When emotional upheavals happen in your life, it is an opportunity to examine why you journeyed down that path. It is not the time to form negative core beliefs in a stage of anger.

Remember that what you constantly think about will manifest in your life. If you judge others, you will be judged in the same manner.

Resentment only destroys your quality of life from the inside out. You will be the one who suffers the most and the longest if you grasp tightly to misery.

## *Step Four: Empathize*

For genuine forgiveness to happen, it is necessary for you to place yourself in the shoes of the offender. If you have not forgiven the past, you will automatically respond out of your own personal problems, pain, fears, and experiences. This will lead you to actions that can hurt others.

If you practice kindness toward yourself and others, you will be blessed with inner peace. When you allow negative feelings to overwhelm you, the life you desire to create is sabotaged.

Look at the world through the eyes of kindheartedness and see the goodness in others. It is everywhere you choose to see it.

You are not the sin police. It is not your assignment to manage anyone else's life.

## *Step Five: You Are Free When You Forgive*

You can forgive and still maintain your integrity. Forgiveness does not mean relationships must be restored or that your irritation about an offense is unjustified.

The key is to absolve others for their actions. Grace is not a license to sin. Forgiveness is full of compassion, but demands a change in conduct.

Forgiveness requires dedication and focus. By clinging to your anger, you are unwittingly projecting onto people who have not hurt you, defeating your quest for true love from the start.

What if you can't forgive yourself for something you did to another person? Remember that you must practice forgiveness not only to those who hurt you, but also give grace to yourself.

## He Hurt Me; I Got Back At Him - Now What?

Your natural instinct when someone offends you is to harm the other person back. Maddie and Ted are struggling with trust issues that have damaged their foundation. By exacting her revenge on her boyfriend for seeing someone else, Maddie now realizes that her actions have caused an enormous erosion of faith in each other.

*My partner and I have been together for two years now, but recently it has all started to go wrong. You see, a few months ago, we split up, because we both needed some space. I moved out, but then I found out a couple of days later that he was going with someone else. This really hurt me, but I kept meeting him because I wanted him back. I love him deeply. Then eventually, after a month or so, we got back together. Not long after we were back together, I cheated on him, with someone he knew, in our bed, while he was away on holiday.*

*I was very drunk, and can't remember anything. I denied it while he was away, but he found out as soon as he got home that it was true. He stayed with me, but he was devastated. I regret it with all my heart. Ever since, our relationship hasn't quite been the same. He wants me to tell him exactly what happened, but I can't, because I don't remember.*

*I've tried talking to him, but I have an emotional problem where I can't open up, which has a great deal to do with my past. He gets annoyed with this, but I've tried so hard, the words just don't come out!*

*We constantly dig at each other, and argue. I hate arguing with him. He says he's lost trust in me! And I'm not quite sure if I trust him completely. I truly, truly love him, and couldn't stand to be without him, and I know he loves me, but will we ever be as happy as we used to be? Will he ever trust me again? We both want to stay together, and spend our lives together, but I'm fed up with the arguments!*

Trust has diminished, and it will disappear completely if Maddie does not open up and become vulnerable. Love and faith go hand in hand. She does not love Ted in the true meaning of the word; it is her fear of exposing her emotions and setting herself up for possible heartache that keeps her in with her boyfriend.

She "needs" the feeling that this relationship generates, which is not psychologically healthy. Before they can move forward, both Maddie and Ted must explore their core beliefs and discover why they are attracted to the chaos that they generate as a couple.

Forgiveness is not for the benefit of the person who wronged you. It is for your freedom. For your emotional and spiritual well-being, forgive those who have hurt you and move forward. It is your key to happiness and emotional freedom. Forgiveness provides freedom to live in peace and experience abundance in life and love.

# Chapter Seven
## The Spiritual Battle

*Psychological Awareness Plus Spiritual Maturity Are Key To Successful Relationships*

You are fighting a spiritual battle against the forces of evil that want to keep you from experiencing the tender, caring, and loving relationship God has in store for you.

Part of the combat lies in understanding the intellectual and psychological reasons you are attracted to the people you have selected previously and learning the skills necessary to break those chains of repression.

However, all the knowledge in the world will not get you permanently to this abundant life if you do not fight the good crusade of faith and surrender your life to God.

The second part of this process is building your faith in God and surrendering every aspect of your life—including finding the right partner—to Him.

Trust that He will bless you in His perfect timing with a devoted, respectful partnership when you are ready to receive, accept, and enjoy it.

Your utmost miracles will occur out of your greatest storms of life.

## I *Need* Someone in My Life

Covetousness is a fixation for something you want and believe you need to have in order to be happy or satisfied (such as attracting true love). It is a form of idolatry and has many negative consequences. Once you learn how to identify, confess, and lay down greediness in your life, you can experience all the abundant blessings God has for you, including a well adjusted, happy relationship.

Your spiritual nature needs a connection with God to hear His messages. If you live a reactionary life and allow your emotions to rule your world, you will never encounter the peace and joy that are here for you each day. If you hop on the rollercoaster ride of your emotions, you will live with fear and anxiety, which blocks God from blessing your life, as the two cannot coexist. It is a domino effect; the more you focus on what you don't have and the things you fear and the terrible things that may happen, the more likely that you will bring those things to pass. That is the purpose of surrendering your life to God. He wants to carry your burdens and wants you to trust that His ways are for your spiritual well-being and growth. He wants to be close to you.

## Why Does God Want Me to Surrender?

Total surrender is crucial to receiving God's blessing for you. You may have heard that this is the key to your walk with God, but have you wondered why God desires your submission? What is the purpose? The answer lies in God's desire for an intimate and personal relationship with you through sincere, honest worship. God loves your reverence, and the only way you can offer it to Him is if you are totally surrendered.

How much of your life are you giving to God and how much are you reserving for yourself? As we revisit Mark and Suzanne, we find that Mark has not relinquished to God completely. He is holding on to a relationship he knows is not good for him, but he is tempted by Elaine's passionate desire for him and her pleading to get back together. Since he has not surrendered this part of his life to God, Mark

106

has left the door to his mind open wide to temptation. The lure is the promise of the type of love and passion he believes he deserves. His lack of total trust in God's plan for his life and the issues He is trying to help Mark resolve are in danger of being thwarted.

> *Elaine loves me with such reckless passion - I mean I have never had anyone tell me like she tells me that she's in love with me. It is so incredibly passionate. She's absolutely breathtaking . . . see, she appeals to the poetic, romantic side of me in ways that no one else has, because she does possess certain talents - artistry - that no one else has.*

From a psychological view, Mark is highly attracted to Elaine because the feelings that they generate as a couple remind him of his relations with his mother. He is highly entranced with Elaine because she holds not only the attraction of replaying those old feelings, but also holds the promise of attaining the love he feels he ought to have.

Although his relationship with Suzanne is comparable, he has a better chance of establishing an emotionally strong partnership with her than with Elaine. This is a spiritual battle that requires Mark to yield to God.

Perhaps your anger or grief has become part of your identity and you do not want to liberate it. Perhaps it's a bad habit that you want to hold on to. Or it could be that person you know is nothing but trouble for you. You need to get to the place where you have no conditions on your relationship with God. Otherwise, all of your praying is in vain.

Further conversations with Mark reveal his deeper feelings for Elaine. He does not yet realize how close he is to running back to her. His self-image is flattered, and that is blinding him to God's will. Even if he stays with Suzanne and marries her, he will risk losing everything if he does not shut the door to the temptation he allowed in.

*The reason I say it frightens me is that I am scared that I am supposed to react to such passion. Is this is the love that I am entitled to? I want someone to love me with reckless abandon because it's exciting and wonderful. However, something tells me in my gut that this isn't real, that she would revert to her old ways. And, then where am I?*

*Please tell me my gut is right and that I am not pushing away the love of my life. I have always held this fear that if I went back to Elaine that I would be right back where I was with her. She would sense I was getting too close again and back way away again. Tell me my gut is right on that.*

Mark's intuition (God) is telling him what he already knows to be true. His mind says the opposite. By holding on to parts of your life, you are telling God that you do not completely trust His judgment, good intentions, and will for your life. You are telling the Creator of the universe that you know better in these areas of your life. If you do not trust God, you do not really love Him, and your ability to be personal with Him is blocked. Through surrender, you will discover God's will.

## If I Surrender, I Lose Myself

Human nature is fearful of the unknown, especially when asked to hand over control of our lives. Do you assume that your life will be limited or held back if you take the leap of faith and allow God to fight your battles? Are you apprehensive about God's will for your life?

We are usually more prepared to accept bad things that happen to us than to believe for the very best, the abundant life that only God can provide.

There will be times when what you perceive to be the best path to follow is not what God has in mind for you. He sees the road ahead where you can't see. His vision is not limited, but yours is. Challenges will still arise in your life, but by placing your unconditional trust in God, you will have peace in your heart that His plan offers the most abundant, rewarding way of all.

## I Feel Defeated, Bitter and Alone

Nona has come to realize that her struggle in love is a spiritual battle. Her father was emotionally absent when she was a child. He turned to alcohol to handle the stress of life, further distancing himself from Nona. This family curse goes back many years. But Nona has the power to break this chain of events if she surrenders to God and trusts Him.

*I had a four year relationship with a man who lied and cheated repeatedly. I've now just been dumped after three years with a man who had a long distance relationship going on for most of the time we were together. This last guy has really messed me up. He's really a good guy. He knew about my past experience and since he'd been cheated on by his ex-girlfriend, he swore he'd never do this to me.*

*He was very loving, caring, affectionate, and seemed to have total respect for me and my feelings. His friends, family, and I are all totally shocked that he deceived me like this. He informed me we were splitting by leaving a message on my answering machine! When we finally got to talk, he said he'd been "dropping hints for months" but I still don't know what those hints were. He told me "you'll get over it" and "lots of people go through this" He was cold and sort of heartless. This is so totally out of character for him.*

*It's been about five months now and I'm still reeling from all this. I'm so hurt and angry and bitter I can hardly stand it. I'm trying to stay busy, doing things I used to enjoy but now get no satisfaction from them. I've had several men ask me out but it's too much effort to pretend I'm having a good time. I'm not!*

*I don't think a single day has gone by that I haven't cried. I know that time heals all wounds, but in the mean time this bitterness is destroying every aspect of my life. I just feel angry and hateful towards everyone and everything. I'm lonely and want to get out and do things, but when I do I get angry and depressed watching other people who are happy. What happened?*

*I thought things were going well and we were really connecting. Was it the wrong timing? What do I do to make myself feel better? I feel like there's something wrong with me, like I'm worthless.*

While it is perfectly normal to go through a period of mourning for the loss of love, there is danger in allowing the grief continue and becomes how you define yourself. This is the spiritual battle you face. Through self-pity, your soul gets distracted from fulfilling your God-given destiny and living an abundant and rewarding life.

God brings every person and event into your life for your higher good. Nona's breakup highlights an ongoing spiritual war that God wants to liberate her from. He does not want her to lose this opportunity by becoming depressed, bitter, angry, and envious of everyone and everything. He wants her to forgive what has happened previously. She has a primary belief that the men she loves will eventually leave, either emotionally or through affairs outside of a commitment (which is another form of emotional abandonment).

Through forgiveness of the past, surrender to God, and trusting His will, she will be set free of this painful cycle.

But before God can work in Nona's life, she must let go of her anger. Keep in mind that there are only two emotions: fear and love. God is all love. Everything else is not from God. He cannot work in your life if you are filled with fear and the by-products of anger, depression, and bitterness.

The ending of a relationship is not the end of you. When God closes a door, it is for a reason. He always has a better and brighter door to open for you if you surrender to Him and allow Him to work in your life.

Do you trust that God wants the best for you?

*What then shall we say to these things? If God is for us, who can be against us?* Romans 8:31(NKJV)

God is forever on your side. He has a plan for you. During times of trials, you may not like what is happening, but God will turn every circumstance for your higher good if you do not cave in to the negativity surrounding you.

Allow God to lead the way and reveal the areas He wants to refine in your life. You belong to God. He created you and saved you, and it is your duty to live according to His will.

You must surrender everything to Him to receive the abundance He generously and adoringly wants to bestow on you.

Your outlook through the storms of life will determine your destiny. You may have faced many unfair, unhappy situations in your life, but the pain of today will manifest into the victory of tomorrow if you stay calm and rise above your relationship challenges.

If you are in the middle of a relationship storm, here are a few thoughts to weather the turbulence.

## Remember Your Purpose and Your Calling

The dreams in your heart are uniquely yours and it is God's desire to see you fulfill those promises. He wants to bless you with love with the right person, but you must be ready to receive that gift.

If you have not worked through the trials that repeat in love, you are not prepared. What you do in the midst of the storm of a failed relationship makes all the difference.

Your actions and attitudes will determine whether you win or lose and how quickly you will realize your goal. You cannot control the actions of your ex-boyfriend or ex-girlfriend, but you do have the power to choose your reaction.

## Allow Jesus to Be Your Guiding Force

You must follow your intuition and allow it to dominate the voice the outside world. If you search your spirit, you will recognize the Holy Spirit talking to you, and He will show you what to do and how to avoid loss and harm and disaster in your life.

Follow His lead and do not be moved by circumstances. Be patient and wait on God. Do not allow your emotions to rule your choices. Allow God to direct your steps, and obey His voice when He tells you not to go down the same path. He knows the end from the beginning in your life, in every situation.

## Do Not Be Defined by Emotional Baggage

Storms are perfect times to lighten your emotional load and examine your life. Why? Because emotional storms brew in your life to get your attention and face issues that you avoid otherwise. A crisis is God's way of redirecting your path and getting you focused on His will for your life.

## Keep an Attitude of Hope and Expectancy

There are no hopeless situations if you know Jesus. Although heart-break is painful and can seem like the end of the world, it truly is a new beginning. When God closes a door He always opens a better and brighter one. All you need to do is stop looking at the closed door and see the one that He opened especially for you. He is always there for you, particularly during the darkest times.

## Share Your Pain with Others

Refuse to become self-centered and isolated during the trials. The best way to redirect your focus is to help someone else in his or her time of need. When you are upset and in emotional turmoil, your human nature wants to dwell on the pain. The last thing you want to do during a crisis or breakup is help out others. You may be tempted to throw a pity party and invite all your friends. I assure you, that road only leads to prolonging your misery.

The challenge is to ask, "What do I have in my hand?" You may look at yourself and the circumstances around you and conclude that you have nothing to give. That is the wrong answer, as every person has something to give, especially when going through tribulations. You may feel as if you are holding on by your fingernails, but if you boldly seek out a need and fill it, you will find God's power in your seemingly empty hand.

When you are hurt emotionally, you may believe that the timing to help others is not convenient, but God will ask you to give away the very thing you need. You need love? God will ask you to give away your love. When we give, God takes what we give and does exceeding abundantly more than we could ask or think. <sup>Ephesians 3:20(NKJV)</sup>. You may think that the little things you give look small compared to the great need. But God can use your willing heart to make a big difference in someone else's life. There is more happiness in giving than in receiving. <sup>Acts 20:35(AMP)</sup>

Each relationship that ends has a lesson for you. It is never about the other person. The secret is to examine why you attracted this person into your life. Work on those issues.

By going through this experience, you are a valuable witness for others in the same situation. If you give what is in your hand, your pain will be rewarded with beauty.

# Chapter Eight
## Power over Your Thoughts

## *Stopping the Downward Spiral of Negative Thoughts*

Attracting the right partner starts with showing your true, authentic self to others. Pretenses keep you concealed from people. No one can see who you are when you are hiding your vulnerability. As long as your attention is in the present, and your intent for the future is clear, you are on the path to manifesting the right relationship.

Many people have created defenses in order to "protect" themselves from potential hurt and heartbreak. The downside to this rationale is that the person you want to attract cannot find you behind the mask. If you cling to your barricade, you will attract superficial people, who look good on the outside but do not offer emotional and spiritual fulfillment.

Our thoughts have creative power. Every consideration, action, and word generates a force of energy that returns to us in kind. Truly what you sow is what you reap, as each seed begins as a thought in your mind. What you think and say you will also reap.

Each moment presents choices for you to make. Some you make reflexively because core beliefs are so ingrained that you believe they are truths. Some choices you make fully aware of the consequences, ignoring the voice of your intuition. The key is to stay in the present moment and learn to select paths that bring blessings to you as well as to others. If you say or do something that brings hurt, pain, or deception to another, you will bring in that harvest eventually.

Your mind, intellect, will, and emotions will justify what your intuition condemns. Your spirit is always at battle with your carnal mind. It is your responsibility to retrain yourself to listen to your intuition and hear the wisdom and direction of God. The false thoughts you have created about yourself will always fight for control of your mind and the routes you take in life.

If you do not love and value yourself, no one in your life will ever be able to fill that void. You cannot attract a strong, stable relationship if you do not love and appreciate yourself. When you feel worthwhile, you possess a positive self-image.

## Where Did I Learn to Be So Self-Critical?

If your parents made you feel loved and respected, you felt comfortable and safe in your home and surroundings. If you were not raised in a loving environment, and were criticized excessively, you probably felt unlovable. This feeling may have followed you to school, where you felt rejected by your peers or unable to compete in sports or the class-room.

As we grow up, our minds create tapes of the impressions others have of us, some of which are flawed. Because we hear criticism the same way we hear praise, the negative opinions we hear, especially from those we are emotionally vulnerable to, can damage our self-esteem. It is difficult to keep the disapproval we hear from family and close friends in perspective when we have so much on the emotional line with those individuals.

It is important to remember that "constructive criticism" has nothing to do with you. It is usually about the issues that person is failing to face in his or her own life. Each time you are faced with a situation that reminds you of one of these damaging tapes, your buttons get pushed and you react to the present event with the same intensity as when you first experienced that feeling.

You draw people into your intimate life to push these buttons and heal the pain you have avoided. It is God's way of allowing you to face your darkness, learn how to forgive, and stop allowing your past to define who you are today. It is a matter of becoming more conscious of your reactions and exploring the reasons behind your intense emotions.

Are you allowing deeply-rooted ideas to rule your relationships today?

When you allow self-criticism to take over your thoughts, you have a sense of powerlessness in relationships and your daily life circumstances. Life is overwhelming for you. The nature of self-criticism is to mask self-doubts. A life not surrendered to God rides on a rollercoaster of emotions, with feelings of adequacy and inadequacy co-existing or changing frequently.

There are ten unconscious motivations for self-criticism:

- To motivate ourselves to do better
- To keep ourselves humble
- To avoid doing something challenging
- To avoid disappointments; that is when you fear failure
- To discourage others from criticizing us
- To encourage others to admit their faults too
- To avoid responsibility—"Don't expect much from me"
- To imply we have superior standards by saying our behavior was beneath us, not reflective of our true abilities
- To get sympathy and reassurance
- To express other feelings indirectly, such as anger or guilt or a need to be in a subordinate position within the family.

Your internal critic blames you when things go wrong (and you accept the blame). When things go well, you call it luck or say, "Someone felt sorry for me." Expressing self-criticism and self-blame may relieve some tension, but in the end you are degraded. Likewise, you may feel good about setting high perfectionist standards, but in the end you fail because you can't be perfect. The critic in your mind constantly tells you how inadequate you are, especially in comparison to "the best." If you attack yourself, maybe others won't attack, but in the end you dislike yourself. This critic isn't honest; it exaggerates your failures. It remembers all your mistakes and sins and calls you names. The critic may be such a natural, ordinary part of your mental life that you may hardly notice the criticism or the damage done.

A low self-concept may be responsible for defeatist "giving up" or for obsessive workaholic behavior. A negative self-concept may result in constant self-put-downs or in constantly trying to prove one's superiority. People with low self-esteem may be over-attentive, giving, and solicitous, believing that no one will like them unless they are super nice, or they may be hostile and offensive, rejecting the other person first.

Let's examine four self-critical attitudes that result in a feeling of powerlessness.

## 1) There's nothing I can do.

This attitude is one of self-destructiveness, self-sabotage, or self-hatred. It may turn your anger toward yourself. If you sabotage yourself, you will suffer from the fear of success, low self-esteem, and a preoccupation with evaluating life situations and convincing yourself that you are incompetent to deal with whatever is at hand.

Psychoanalysts have long believed that anger toward others gets turned against us. Anger converted into self-hatred can cause depression. The basic problem starts with parents who are inconsistent (either overindulgent or demanding), lacking in warmth, inconsiderate or openly hostile, or driven by their own needs. The child resents these things. But parents are powerful and a child's only means of survival. So, because of fear or love or guilt, the child represses the anger. The child, being small, alone, confused, and helpless in an unpredictable, hostile world, is, of course, scared. How does the child protect himself?

The child, aware of his or her weakness, the criticism of others, and his or her own hostility and fears, develops a "despised" self-concept. The resentment of others is also turned against the self: "I am unlovable, a bad person." At the same time, the child starts to develop a notion of an "ideal" self—what he or she should be—in order to survive and get the love and approval he or she wants. This ideal self, trying to compensate for weakness and guilt, sets up impossible demands, called neurotic needs. These needs are unconscious, intense, insatiable, anxiety-causing, and out of touch with reality.

In extreme cases, some people become so self-effacing, compliant, unselfish, and modest they almost do away with their "self." Suffering, helplessness, and martyrdom are their ideals. They need to be loved, liked, approved, important, but taken care of. Their "conclusion" is: *"If you love me, you will not hurt me."* But beneath this saintly surface lies anger, rage, and strong urges to be aggressive and mean. Because love is never perfect, these kinds of dejected people may turn against themselves, becoming very self-critical and unhappy. Often they become bitter because their unwritten rule was broken; namely, *"I'll be nice and not hate you if you will love, respect, and care for me always."* People striving for sainthood often suffer because others do not always put them first.

Recognizing yourself as the cause of your misery and limitations can lead to shame. If you accept that there is nothing you can do, you may avoid attempting to do anything. The more out of control you feel the fewer internal resources you possess to make life decisions.

Robin allows her negative thoughts to overpower her, which affects all areas of her life, from her family life to her romantic life to her work environment. Because Robin's self-esteem is so low, she unconsciously sabotages her advancement in her career. She plays the martyr at work, believing that her boss is against her.

> *I try and do well at work, yet my boss doesn't see it. He left me out of a busi-*

*ness deal recently. Everyone in my department has defended me.*

*They keep telling my boss what an asset I am, yet he is taking his advice from someone who doesn't even work in my department. I can't take it personally but I just feel my bad energy is encapsulating the earth.*

*I think I am a good, honest, caring, trustworthy hardworking person. But I hate myself because no one else seems to think I am worthwhile. I don't know how to change their perception of me.*

Robin feels helpless at work. She has a fundamental belief that she is unworthy. You cannot believe in yourself and hate yourself at the same time. If negative thoughts rule your mind, you will be viewed in that light.

If some relatively minor event has saddened you—and you have stayed down too long, you must examine your conclusions about that event. Remember that depressed people demand too much sometimes, get obsessed with a loss, blame themselves (no benefit of the doubt), let events get them down, and don't think they can do anything about the depression.

That is the nature of depression and low self-esteem. They see no silver lining, no light at the end of the tunnel, no opportunity for growth in this crisis. They aren't thinking rationally.

## 2) I didn't try hard enough.

Healthy, useful guilt is the feeling we have when we do something we rationally judge to be morally wrong or unfair. Just having the thought or urge to do something bad can cause guilt. That is good if it keeps us from doing something inconsiderate. Healthy guilt is our reasonable, fair conscience. But there is unhealthy guilt too. That is when we establish unreasonable standards for ourselves. We expect perfection, want to accomplish the impossible, feel responsible for misfortunes in other people's lives, and believe we are "good" only if we faithfully follow all the rules and do more than required. This guilt does not allow for mistakes; we expect too much from ourselves and others.

Self-pity may begin with an early significant trauma. It can become an unconscious method of self-comforting in order to deal with this experience. Seeing yourself as powerless, you may try to control your compulsive behaviors. One of your core beliefs is, *"If I am to blame for my failure because I didn't try hard enough, then I must try harder to increase my authority."*

Robin experienced emotional trauma early in life. She is part of a cycle of emotional abuse that started with her grandmother's treatment of her mother:

> *My mother came from an abusive home. My grandmother was divorced and my grandmother sent my mom and aunt to live with either their grandmother or an orphanage. When they were at home, they were mentally abused. One time my grandmother left a note for them to see when they got home from school. The note said, "I can't stand you girls anymore. I have left and you need to take care of yourselves." They were about seven and ten years old. She then crawled out from under the bed laughing.*
>
> *So growing up I felt abandonment I think. My mother criticized me a lot. To this day, I hate the way I look. I have always felt ugly (I think honestly I am, just don't*

> *want to accept it). I remember a man tell-*
> *ing me when I was about fourteen,*
> *"You're so ugly, you're cute." I will*
> *NEVER forget that. I have always felt my*
> *mother didn't like me as much as my*
> *brother because he is very handsome. I*
> *have always felt I was a failure.*

Robin has such a negative view of herself, both internally and exter-
nally, that the hatred she has for herself is revealed through her physical
appearance. Her challenge will be to break this self-hatred cycle so she
does not pass this curse of her family down to another generation.

The depressed person has been preprogrammed to think negatively and
irrationally. This is not a conscious, intentional effort to come to
negative conclusions; it is an automatic process. You just assume your
negative thinking is right because you have always thought that way
and no one has challenged your thinking.

For example, when a depressed person feels self-critical, his or her
unreasonable thought is, *I can't do anything right.* The reasonable
thought when feeling self-critical is *I made a mistake, but I can do
better.*

## 3) This is impossible to do.

This feeling of helplessness leads you to believe that others are to
blame for your powerlessness. Outside forces are the cause, and you
believe you are not accountable for the situations in your life. You
believe that life isn't fair. You might give in to the fear of authority
figures, believing they require the impossible from you. You paint
yourself as a victim in life.

> *My mother lives in another country.*
> *When she was visiting me, we went out to*
> *dinner. After a few drinks she asked if I*
> *blamed her for how she treated me when*

*I was young. She said she didn't know how important it was to give me praise and appreciation. She says she feels responsible for my lack of self esteem.*

*I told her I did not blame her and we all only do the best with what we know at the time. We have been getting along much better now and I do feel she loves me. Before I've always felt that I was a disappointment and she hated me.*

*I still feel very inadequate. She helps me with my makeup and hair and although I appreciate her help, it makes me feel like I'm so ugly.*

Robin feels overwhelmed by her lack of self-confidence. She mentally understands that her mother is a product of her environment and the treatment she received from her mother as a young child. But in her heart, Robin does not trust her own words. She thinks she is a disappointment as a daughter, sister, and employee. She is so consumed with her fears that she doesn't know how to undo her core beliefs and thus resigns herself to a life of ugliness.

## 4) I can't succeed because I'm unlucky.

This attitude toward life is defined by feelings of self-pity and a belief that circumstances are beyond your control. If you believe in luck rather than God and allow feelings of self-pity to take over your emotions, your life satisfaction will be low.

*I was engaged to be married to my high school boyfriend until I found out he was cheating on me. He then begged me to stay, saying he didn't think I loved him enough. This pattern continues for many years until he finally left me for good.*

*That was a few years ago and my life seems to just keep going downhill. I have dated some guys since then, but no one to be proud of. Most have lived out of town, or are much younger than me. I recently broke up with a man who has a felony record for traveling across state lines with drugs, lives with his cousin and is NOT someone I would introduce to anyone. Yes, I stayed with him for over two years.*

*Lately, I date less. I have been having more plastic surgery and things in my life are not good. I have many good things but I'm still unhappy. I'm trying to date online, but no one of any character writes to me. Where should I start? It is hard for me to change my energy.*

*I will try to improve and feel better for a short time. But as soon as something negative happens like getting hits on my dating site from only horrible, horrible men, or like this thing at work, I feel defeated and ask myself why should I even try? Nothing is going right no matter how much surgery I have to improve my looks or how hard I try at work!*

Robin sees these issues as separate, but they are truly one. She attracts men who will reflect her core belief that she is unworthy and ugly, and she will continue to do so until she makes a bold effort to change her thought life.

## Recognizing the Barriers to Positive Self-Image

Sometimes we view changes, even self-improvements and career advancements, more daunting than fulfilling. A person may feel fairly content day to day, but over a period of time become concerned that he or she unable to improve his or her life.

There are two kinds of barriers to change:

- It is comfortable to just stay the way you are.
- Fear of getting out of your comfort zone.

This comfort with yourself can be problematic, as the traits you might want to change have become part of your self-concept. You may not like certain characteristics about yourself, but they are an established, permitted part of you.

Your self-concept develops over time, and any challenge to your self-view is threatening. For instance, if a normally mild-tempered person flies into a rage, he may say, *"I wasn't myself."* We protect our self-concept. There is a tendency to continue acting out our self-concept, which inhibits the change we desire.

Let's examine several fears that also inhibit change:

## The fear of growing up

As we outgrow our relaxed, self-pleasing habits of childhood, we are expected to become more reasonable, responsible, and mature. Being an adult may mean giving up an easy life: working steadily, exercising self-control, taking care of others, being assertive, overcoming shyness, and making sure things get done, for example. These changes can be intimidating.

## The fear of success

If you prove you can do something well, people will expect it of you all the time. Show you can fix delicious meals and you'll be asked to make them often. Show you can take write well and you will become the secretary. Show you can calculate numbers in your head and you will become the accountant.

If you are successful, you may acquire more responsibilities and expose yourself to possible failures. Be successful on the job and you will be given more to do. Do well in school and you will be expected to continue to do well until you do poorly. Be successful in love and you are in jeopardy of being left.

## The fear of excelling

Psychologist Dr. Abraham Harold Maslow, who studied self-actualizers, thought that many of us fear and dislike successful people and, thus, we may be reluctant to become great.[ii] Consider how often we hear someone's achievement degraded: *"Wonder how he got so much--probably his family had money"* or *"I'd have lots of friends too if I had a car like that"* or *"Anyone could make all A's if all they did was study."* These remarks of reasonable goals are envious comments. This kind of thinking might reduce one's drive to achieve one's own potential.

## The fear of knowing

Many people would be reluctant to find out their spouses were unfaithful or breaking the law. Once you know, you may have to take action. If you don't know, you don't need to do anything. Likewise, people avoid finding out what is wrong with a person lying on the sidewalk. Knowing the situation requires a person to do something because ignorance can no longer be used as an excuse. Discovering a problem at work or knowing a better solution to a problem than the boss knows can sometimes be scary. Drinkers, smokers, overeaters, procrastinators, and insulters don't want to know the eventual results of their behaviors. We use defense mechanisms to keep from knowing the truth about ourselves.[iii]

## Why Is Change So Difficult?

We all have strong tendencies to resist core change. Most people go through life on automatic pilot, repeating habits of thinking, feeling, relating, and doing over a lifetime. These patterns are comfortable and familiar and are unlikely to change unless there is a concerted, deliberate, and sustained effort to do so. Mistakes repeat unless there is an intentional attempt to alter them. Most people avoid situations and feelings that cause pain, even when confrontation leads to growth. In order to change, you must be willing to face situations you have avoided most of your life.

To attract a positive relationship, you must retrain your mind to stop your inner critic. When you choose to dwell on the negative people, situations, or events in your life, you are blocking God from blessing your life abundantly.

Your thoughts are the mirror to your soul. How you think is revealed through how you act and speak. *"For as he thinks in his heart, so is he "* Proverbs 23:7(NKJV)

The more life you give your situation, the stronger it becomes until it eventually takes root in your soul. Each time a negative thought enters your mind, remember that the enemy is trying to gain control of your life through your most vulnerable areas. When your psyche starts down a negative path, consciously stop yourself from getting caught up in that line of thinking and cast it out.

It takes time to change a habit and more time to incorporate a new habit into your lifestyle. Give yourself a few weeks and concentrate on releasing any unconstructive thoughts and any temptation to speak disapprovingly about yourself and/or your situation.

Until you can uncover the lesson behind recurring situations and understand their meaning, similar people and situations will replay in your life. Paying attention to negative messages that stunt personal and spiritual growth leads to identifying what prevents you from living a blessed, abundant life in God's will.

## *Count It All Joy: A Biblical Solution for Self-Criticism*

Your attitude either draws people toward you or repels them. It is a choice you make and it is never based on circumstances. Your mind-set toward love is vital. You must maintain a positive outlook in order to draw constructive people into your life. The Bible makes many references to the significance of your outlook in all circumstances.

> *My brethren, count it all joy when you fall into various trials, knowing that the testing of your faith produces patience. But let patience have its perfect work, that you may be perfect and complete, lacking nothing.* James 1:2-4(NKJV)

Stop defining yourself by your past sorrow and set backs, and count it all joy. Every circumstance is an opportunity to grow closer to God and strengthen your relationship with Him. Nothing is impossible with our God, as all things work together for good to those who love God, to those who are the called according to *His* purpose. Romans 8:28(NKJV)

You have the power to turn your problems into blessings. It's all about how you look at what has happened to you. You will never appreciate the gift of love without experiencing the depths of heartache and pain at love lost. With a resilient attitude, you can turn your past pain into future success.

Kylee has developed a habit of labeling life experiences as negative. Her vision is clouded by fearful thoughts of her love not being reciprocated and not being accepted by those she loves. Kylee does not love herself, so she inflicts as much ugliness towards others as possible. Her attitude and behavior prevents the love she desperately seeks from boyfriends, family and friends. Instead of bringing those she loves closer, she drives them off, only to wish them back. She knows she is a sweet and considerate person at heart, but the depth of her self-loathing brings out the angry, scared child who still mourns the loss of her parent's marriage.

*My boyfriend and I broke up three months ago. I can't stop thinking about him and I keep on telling myself that I need to stop. However, I feel like it's not really over. The last time we talked he said that maybe years from now we could be together, which I agree. I'm a co-dependant and I think he used to be, but he learned the hard way too. He had a girlfriend that stomped on his heart and he has been dead inside for seven years going from barfly to barfly, then he met me at work. I'm nothing like his ex girl-friends. I'm nice, sweet, and considerate. I have good morals. He said that he was dead inside until he met me. After we started going out I never felt better and we wanted to be together all the time.*

*Everything was great until I started having problems with him because of how I was feeling at the time. I have break-downs from time to time so I rely on other people to make me happy. He was-n't making me happy anymore so I started being really nasty to him and basically showing him that he wasn't doing any-thing right. I felt like I was giving so much in the relationship, but I wasn't get-ting anything back. I was making sure that he was happy while putting my needs second. I know it wasn't his fault.*

*I really miss him and I want to know if you think I may have another chance with him or how I may get him back. I'm not contacting him because I'm trying not to look needy. I'm not waiting around for him either. I felt so comfortable around him and he really truly knew me and I feel like we belong together, like I waited my whole life for somebody like him. I talk to other guys, but I just don't feel it with them.*

As Kylee has experienced, there is always struggle before success in every aspect of life, and love is no exception. You have the choice to look at your past as an opportunity to learn and grow emotionally and spiritually or as an obstacle to love. The person who never made a mistake in relationships is the person who never tried to find real love. In order to love others, you must first love yourself. There is no person, place, circumstance, event or any other external thing that will bring inner peace and happiness.

The spiritual battle Kylee faces is stopping the work of the enemy in her life. All her self-destructive feelings are habitual conditioned choices. She has developed this reaction in an attempt to protect herself from getting emotionally hurt. She chooses not to see the blessing in each experience which blocks God from trading the ashes of her past pain for the beauty He longs to give her.

*I just want to know why I push people away. I do it all the time. That's what I did with my ex and all of my friends. I was fine in my life and I never could have been happier until I started puberty. I was popular and good looking and I had a lot of friends. I got acne and I used makeup to cover it up. People started to make fun of me and I never felt worse.*

*I was uncomfortable going to school and that's when I discovered food. Not only did I have acne but I started to get fat too. I was getting made fun of everyday. The only people I felt comfortable around were my friends and family. Then my parents got divorced and my whole family pretty much split up and everything was so different. Then my friends dumped me because they said that I was just being a complete bitch. I didn't think I was but that is how I am.*

*Once I meet someone I'm excited to be around them, then I get bored start making fun of them to entertain myself. I put others down too for my own amusement. So I didn't have any friends or a close-knit family anymore and I felt miserable. After that I started thinking about things that I never thought about before. I started to think that I wasn't interesting enough because I thought I could get my friends back but all I wanted to do was act like myself, but I didn't know who that was anymore because my friends made me feel horrible for being myself. I have bad social skills. I don't like school or anything that reminds me of it.*

*I have breakdowns whenever I get those feelings back and that's usually every other year. I was fine when I just hung out with my Mom and had friends but not friends that I got real close with. I got tired of relying on people because I always felt like they let me down. That's why I think I don't like to get close to people because I have the fear of losing them. It consumes me and all I do is worry.*

*When I first started to go out with my boyfriend everything was great and fun and new. Then I started to get used to him and I felt like I had to impress him all of the time or he'd leave me. I started to worry and fear losing him. I hated how I felt. I felt like I was going nuts. All I do is think and I have thoughts racing in my head all of the time and I just want it stopped.*

*When I don't think, I'm great. My inner voice wants me to be miserable just because it can do it. I feel like I drive people away is just because I can. If I do certain things I know it will drive them away so I do them. Kind of like a test to see how loyal they are to me and then I start to hate them because I feel like its not my fault I'm like this and that they want so much from me and they only like me because of how I act at times. Let's just say that I don't act the same all the time. This is what I always worried about if I would ever get into a relationship. I think too much and therefore I try to form myself into what people want, but I change from day to day.*

*I just want to be myself and that was what I was like mainly with him, but I just got so used to him and bored with him that I didn't really make any effort for him to stay interested in me. I love him though and I just don't think I knew it then. We broke up once before, but since we worked together then, I was able to reel him in again. I feel like if I would have still worked with him then we would still be together. I just want him back.*

In order to experience love, Kylee must forgive her parents for breaking up the family when they divorced, forgive herself for her behavior and seek the guidance and wisdom only God can provide. By learning to place her life in the palm of God's hands and surrendering her will, she can begin the journey to building her self-worth and esteem.

Everything in life that is important involves taking chances. To love is to risk not being loved back, but not to take a chance on love is a life filled with emptiness.

# ·Part Two Exercise·

What pain are you holding in your heart?

Describe the incident and those involved in detail from your perceptive at the time. Then take a step back and examine the situation from your perspective now.

The pain/grudges/resentment I have towards my parents originated with the following incident:


How I perceive what happened:


How they perceive what happened:


What my perspective is today and how it is affecting my relationships today:


The pain/grudges/resentment I have towards my sibling(s) originated with the following incident:


How I perceive what happened:


How they perceive what happened:

134

What my perspective is today and how it is affecting my relationships today:



The pain/grudges/resentment I have towards my friend originated with the following incident:



How I perceive what happened:



How they perceive what happened:



What my perspective is today and how it is affecting my relationships today:



What critical messages does your mind tell you on a daily basis?



What are the origins of those messages and what triggers your self-critical voice?



Describe areas of your life where you feel your critical voice has limited your opportunities:

In your personal life:


My positive affirmation to counter this negative thought is:


The scripture reference I use to reinforce my stance against this negative thought:


In your education:

My positive affirmation to counter this negative thought is:


The scripture reference I use to reinforce my stance against this negative thought:


In your career choices:


My positive affirmation to counter this negative thought is:


The scripture reference I use to reinforce my stance against this negative thought:

In your friendships:

My positive affirmation to counter this negative thought is:



The scripture reference I use to reinforce my stance against this negative thought:



In your family life:

My positive affirmation to counter this negative thought is:



The scripture reference I use to reinforce my stance against this negative thought:



In order to experience all the abundance that Jesus wants to give you in every area of your life, you must fight these self-critical thoughts. If you do not address and overcome these negative thoughts, you will not fulfill your destiny to its fullest measure. Your gifts and talents and creativity will be stunted because of the fear this wrong thinking produces.

You do have the power to take captive every negative thought and turn it around into a positive affirmation. Remember that everything good is from God, as He is the source of love.

On a daily basis, recognize the reoccurring themes to your self-critical thoughts. Write down the areas that are attacked on a regular basis and counter them with positive affirmations.

I encourage you to say your affirmation out loud, as hearing your own voice speaking powerful, positive words will take hold in your soul. If you are proactive and take action as soon as these negative thoughts appear, you can overcome these false limitations once and for all.

# Part Three

# How to Attract the "Right One"

In Part Three, How To Attract the "Right One" the right relationship will manifest when you take action and describe the type of qualities that person possesses.

Once you have defined your close relationships – from parents to friends to romantic partners – you will then begin to see meaningful, fulfilling and puposeful relationships flourish.

Chapter Nine

# Chapter Nine
# The Relationship Plan

## Creating Your Ideal Relationships

Attracting the right relationship partner starts with allowing others to see your true self without any pretense. You must release any façade that keeps your emotional vulnerability protected and hidden. You cannot draw the ideal person until you uncover your authentic self.

Once your focus is in the present and your intent for the future is clear, you are then on course to allowing God to bring this person to you. It is through your faith in God and in His perfect will and perfect timing that brings your desire to reality.

Your life will get out of balance when your main focus is not on God. Allowing anything (career, money, advancement, material possessions) or anyone (or the search for that person) to come between you and God is counterproductive behavior.

The conscious mind requires a focal point of reference on what you want to achieve in life. A Relationship Plan is a tool to discipline your mind from straying from your dreams into negative territory. With practice you can retrain your mind from thinking unconstructive thoughts. The Relationship Plan is a powerful means to meet your goals as it allows you to distinctly define your priorities and primary relationships.

A clear vision of the person you want in your life is necessary to maintain in your conscious mind. There is no need to obsess over the date, place, and time. The main purpose of each day is to live with a positive attitude, knowing that you are one day closer to meeting that special person. Be grateful for the events and people that you are blessed to enjoy each day. A wasted life is one that lives for tomorrow and neglects the wonders, joy, and lessons of the present moment.

A Relationship Plan creates a visual image of being the person you say you are, void of pretense. It is a reminder of the positive characteristics you possess and the boundaries you place with family and friends and those you interact with on a daily basis.

Outlining all the significant relationships in your life is essential, as your core beliefs can show up anywhere. Generally you will see the highest manifestation in your intimate relationships, but those beliefs will also appear to varying degrees in your interactions at school, at work, in friendships, and with family members.

The Relationship Plan is a characterization of your relationship with God and your faith in His divine plan for your life. It also serves as a visual guide for your conscious mind to see the type of person you desire for a future marriage partner. It is intended as a means to live your life fully, out of your vision of your "ideal self," and to rely on God for His security and support to keep it ever-present.

The first step of the Relationship Plan describes your ideal self. The "Who I Am" section gives a declaration of self, much like a mission statement. It outlines the most significant realms of your life from which this self-described "self" emerges.

Within each realm you will choose specific actions and describe their intended results, which will allow you to fully experience this vision of yourself in your present-day reality.

As a result, you will cut the strings that define the "old" you and limit your life. You will learn to create and fulfill your own destiny in God's perfect will and timing.

## "Who I Am" Mission Statement

Imagine that you are talking to yourself as your own best ally, a friend who knows you inside and out who knows every fear, worry, painful event, and unhappy relationship outcome, and who knows what you truly long for. A friend who loves you and knows the life you want to lead.

What would that friend tell you? Write out the one statement that your "friend" sees as an overall view of your life, and create a mission statement to title this part of your Relationship Plan.

Under that statement, list several brief sentences that sum up what that mission statement means to you and how it manifests in your life. Write each sentence in present-tense form: "I am" statements. This is imperative to create the perception in your mind of being this person right now.

The following is an example of a mission statement for a Relationship Plan. Several broad but bold statements are written to give the conscious mind a starting place to spotlight areas to prioritize.

# My Mission Statement

I am living a balanced life, knowing that God is in control.

I live my life dedicated to being the woman God has called me to be and fulfilling His will for my life.

Through my journey with God, I am at peace and emotionally and spiritually fulfilled. My connection with God enables me to have gratifying and meaningful relationships and balance in all areas of my life.

I am free of anxiety and worry and allow God to guide me in my choices in love, career, education, health, recreational activities, friendships and interests.

I choose unlimited abundance and love for myself, my family, my friends and everyone I touch in my life.

After declaring her individual mission statement, Sandra drew an outline of the key realms of her life that her self-described "self" materializes. When you do this for yourself, remember to keep your statements in the present tense.

## My Life Realms

---

1) Relationship with God

2) My Relationship Choices

3) Meaningful Family/Friendship Connections

4) Purposeful Career and Educational Parameters and Goals

5) My Authentic Self

---

Now it is time to address each of the Life Realms in detail and choose specific actions and their intended results. This mental picture will allow you to fully experience this vision of yourself in your present-day reality.

## 1) Relationship with God.

The first question to ask yourself is what you visualize when you think of the ideal connection with God. Write as if it already exists and concentrate on the feelings that come into your heart.

God is not some Higher Power that we call on only when things go wrong - He is there to help us each and every day. He is the Father who wants to bless you with abundance, keep you away from harm and protect you from evil.

By relying on God's plan and purpose for you life, dedicating yourself to obeying His will, you will be able to fulfill the destiny God has specifically determined for you.

## My Relationship with God

I know and have absolute faith that God provides everything in my life. I am comforted by His presence and have peace in my soul.

I am grateful that He gives me the wisdom to make decisions that are pleasing to Him.

I allow God to lead my steps in all areas of my life and have no stress or anxiety about yesterday, today, or tomorrow.

I trust God to lead my surrendered life daily to fulfill His perfect will in my life.

I live a godly life every day, not just on Sunday, and focus my thoughts, words and actions on the things that are pleasing to God.

## 2) *My Relationship Choices.*

Even though most of you are not quite ready to get married yet, it is crucial that you have a solid vision of your future partnership. It is very easy to "fall into" relationships that seem fine – not bad, but not great.

Before you know it, you may end up marrying this person simply because you've been together for a number of years – or subtle peer pressure (all your friends are engaged or married) – or you really have not met anyone better. You may think, "Not me! I would never settle!"

I assure you that countless numbers of my clients have gone down this path and ended up in unfulfilling relationships. You can avoid this altogether by making your declaration of the relationship you desire and allow it to sink into your mind and spirit.

So, imagine you are in the relationship of your dreams. In this section, describe what feelings come to mind in this ideal partnership. Expand on the eventuality of being married to the person God has chosen for you.

## My Relationship Choices

I share a gratifying relationship with a loving man which is based on a strong spiritual connection.

We share our mutual faith and help one another grow stronger spiritually in our walk.

Our foundation is built on mutual love, trust, respect, honor, shared morals, values, and belief in God.

Our union provides me with a firm base that helps me be secure in the secular world. I am unafraid to be the godly woman I know I am each day at home and work.

I communicate clearly with my partner and do not allow anxiety and fear to invade my mind.

Together we plan our future, which includes marriage and children.

### 3) *Meaningful Family/Friendship Connections.*

Fundamental beliefs begin with your parents. Imagine the negativity and problems you face with your family are no longer present.

With that in mind, how would you relate to your parents and siblings? How would you interact to other family members who have fallen out of favor or have been neglected? Tap into those feelings and detail how you see that evolution as if it is happening right now.

Many times the issues we face as a result of our core beliefs are manifested in other close relationships, including friendships. It is important to have boundaries in all your relationships and have a clear picture of the type of people you want as close friends and confidants.

# Meaningful Family/Friendship Connections

I am enjoying a gratifying and satisfying relationship with my parents, and I surrender any negative feelings toward my family to God.

I honor my parents.

I am devoted to keeping my siblings part of my daily life. I refrain from using special occasions as the only times to communicate with them.

We enjoy and build on our friendship as adults and have let the past go.

I am dedicated to my extended family in loving them as a woman of God.

I am forgiving of relatives who push my buttons, and I use those opportunities to rise above any pettiness.

My close friends have a positive outlook on life. They do not bring me down or discourage my dreams. They are supportive, kind and encouraging.

I understand the importance of maintaining friendships and have balance in those relationships. There is an equal amount of give and take in my friendships. I do not take my friends for granted and show them the respect they deserve.

## 4) *Purposeful Career/Educational Parameters and Goals.*

It is important to learn how to achieve a healthy balance between your life and your goals as early as possible. This will serve you well as you launch your career and pursue your dreams.

A life dominated by career and work alone does not leave room for important relationships to flourish and survive. I understand there is a great deal of pressure to be achievement oriented in college. However, this experience is setting the stage for how you conduct yourself on your own.

Your life is more than what you can learn, what you can achieve and how much you can earn. If you do not take the time to learn how to create balance now, you will be extremely tempted to overwork in the beginning of your career. I encourage you to make a conscious effort not to fall into that trap and work your life away.

No one ever looks back at their life and wishes they had spent more time studying or working at the office. If you learn how to establish healthy habits now, you will be mentally and spiritually equipped for life after college.

Leading a life dominated by secular success will not leave you room to pursue the most significant attachment in your life: the one with God. Be clear about setting your priorities and the rest will fall into place.

This is the section to explain those boundaries and create a harmonious and balanced life.

# Purposeful Career/Educational Parameters and Goals

I am pursing the desires of my heart and adding to my knowledge through my chosen field of study.

I am not seeking a career that pleases my parents, relationship partner, society or anyone else. I am following the dreams I have!

I do not listen to people who say I will not be successful in my field or that people with my expertise do not earn enough money to be success-ful. I trust that God will open the right career doors for me as long as I stay true to my calling.

I have set healthy boundaries with my superior in regards to balancing my time at work with uninterrupted time with my partner. My supervi-sor and I enjoy a mutually respectful, professional association, void of anxiety and stress.

I am being utilized in the best possible manner at work and my strong-est talents are called upon to bring the organization to its highest potential.

I am comfortable in my leadership position and have no anxiety toward the opinions and suggestions of others in the workplace. I value their opinions and do not take their words personally.

I am financially secure and know that God provides for all my needs. I am comfortable being an example of a loving woman in the workplace and positively influence the tone and culture of the corporation.

## 5) *My Authentic Self.*

This section is a summary of the person you present to the world. It is the genuine you, without any pretense. You are unashamed of who you are and have a commitment to being this person from day to day, in every environment.

# My Authentic Self

I am at peace with myself and have a clear picture of who I am and the positive characteristics I project to others.

I enjoy each moment and do not hide my vulnerability from others. As a result, I enjoy better personal and career friendships.

I am in control of my thoughts and feelings and enjoy the peace and harmony that occupies the main focus of my mind.

I know how to handle daily stress and put it in proper perspective, knowing that God does not bring any challenge into my life that I cannot handle.

I make time for myself, knowing that I am the best relationship partner, daughter, sister, and friend when I take care of myself physically, mentally, and spiritually.

I am confident in the priorities I set personally and professionally and enjoy a balanced, meaningful, and fulfilling life.

The Relationship Plan outlined above is a guideline for you to use to bring about your preferred life plan with the people around you. This process offers you the means to form a visual image of yourself on the other side of the relationship issues that challenge you now.

I also like to include a special category that describes in detail the ideal person you want to attract into your life—from the characteristics he or she possesses to the feelings you will express to each other. I encourage you to use this image to visualize the unique characteristics your future husband/wife will possess.

God will bring the right person at the perfect time for you, but it is essential that you can identify that person when he or she arrives. The idea behind this method is to let go of the type of person you tend to attract (which continues the cycle you want to break) and direct your heart toward a person with loving, and admirable characteristics.

Here is my personal visual image that I used to attract my husband:

## *My Husband*

*My husband is an independent man who is close to my age, desires children and wants to share the responsibilities, joys and sorrows of life together.*

*A leader that is unconventional in his thinking and actions. He does not follow the crowd.*

*My husband is an extremely romantic, flirtatious, man who notices and compliments me. He never takes me for granted.*

*My husband is passionate and affectionate. He has style, charisma and class.*

*He is fun loving and exciting and enjoys my company.*

*My husband is my best friend.*

*My husband is very handsome and physically fit.*

*My partner is encouraging of my endeavors and dreams.*

*My husband is powerful spiritually.*

*My husband enjoys the performing arts and extensive travel.*

*I am proud to share my husband with family, friends and new acquaintances.*

*I can talk to my husband about anything. We are like minded in our thinking.*

*He has a strong belief in God.*

*He truly desires a harmonious relationship and argues fairly.*

*He loves my family.*

*He likes to shop for and with me and loves my own personal style.*

*My husband spoils me because he enjoys doing so.*

*If he misses me, he tells me.*

*He tells me he loves me on a regular basis.*

*He calls me names of endearment.*

*We will pass our example of a loving relationship to our children, who will marry others who love them in the same manner.*

*My husband is extremely smart, intelligent, well educated, and has a great deal of common sense.*

*He is inspiring to others as well as to me.*

*He is an optimist but a realist.*

*He sees the glass as half full.*

*He is an all-around nice man.*

I suggest that you look over your Relationship Plan on a regular basis to keep it alive in your mind. However, I encourage you not to obsess over it.

Relax. Enjoy each new person you meet and refrain from making snap decisions. Learn to be still and listen to God's wisdom with each new encounter.

# Part Four

# How to Create a Healthy Relationship Foundation

In Part Four, How To Create a Healthy Relationship Foundation, you learn the particulars of communicating your thoughts, needs, desires and dreams to others. Because so many people avoid conflict as much as possible, we will cover how to resolve conflicts in a healthy manner.

It is imperative to go through problems and face each situation as it arises and work towards a solution. Avoidance and procrastination only allows anxiety, worry and fear to escalate to unreasonable levels.

Lastly, we will then discuss the importance of keeping in mind your long range relationship goals concerning children.

# Chapter Ten
## Understanding Your Partner

*Open Up, Share Ideas, Communicate: How to Actively Listen and Hear What's Said*

In a strong, meaningful relationship, you are able to communicate in a positive, loving, and productive manner. This skill takes time to learn, as each person "hears" differently. If we were drawn to people who had our exact strengths and weaknesses, we would miss out on a valuable opportunity to learn tolerance when dealing with others, appreciating differences, expanding our awareness, and opening our hearts to emotional and spiritual growth through diversity. As long as the relationship is built on a solid foundation of shared morals, values, and life goals, these differences will challenge both partners to compromise and adapt to situations that are out of their comfort zone.

In healthy relationships, each person respects and honors his or her partner's communication styles. The way you process information and the manner you assimilate positive and negative communication comprises your communication style. Recognizing your mode and appreciating the method your partner needs to hear and deliver information is essential in effectively getting your point across and being heard.

The most vital aspect of effective communication is learning to listen to your partner. If you only wait for the other person to stop talking so you can say what's on your mind, the lines of communication will break down quickly. Not listening and acknowledging the other person's opinions, lines of thought, points of views and dreams chips away at the trust and connection you have built up as a couple.

If you do not learn how to listen to each other, the commitment will not last. The door to temptation will open as you and/or your partner looks for someone else to connect with emotionally. Effective communication does not completely bypass conflict, as disagreements are part of all well adjusted, functional relationships. Eliminating conflict is not realistic, but understanding each other's thoughts, feelings, and desires and learning how to communicate are the mutual goals.

Be conscious of acknowledging each other's feelings, listening to what is said, and responding accordingly. You will find your bond is strengthened when you are open and truthful.

## How Do I Listen to My Partner?

The main rule for good listening skills involves basic courtesy. It is common for couples to disregard good manners and unintentionally insult each other by not focusing on what's being said.

 Sometimes you do this because you are so ready to resolve the problem at hand and state your own point of view that you forget to listen to what your partner is saying.

Learning the art of listening is vital to maintaining harmony, especially when conflicts arise. The following are rules to be aware of and practice with your loved one.

### 1. Allow your partner to speak uninterrupted.

Do not allow your need to be the problem solver or to be judgmental stop the conversation before it really starts. Your partner is entitled to his or her feelings, whether or not that experience would be a challenge to you in the same situation.

## 2. It is impossible to listen and talk at the same time.

This fundamental rule of effective listening is broken most often. Don't be so eager to add your own views to the conversation and try to interject commentary. Don't wait for a pause in the conversation to jump in. This is rude and irritating and shows a great lack of respect for your partner.

## 3. Stay present.

Some words or topics in conversations will make your mind wander. They place a mental barrier in your mind and you tune out of the conversation. Your partner can see the blank expression in your eyes, signaling that you're not present.

It is important to be conscious of this behavior and discover what makes you check out of conversations and why.

## 4. Eliminate distractions.

Give your loved one your complete attention. Turn off the television, the computer, the cell phone, and stop reading the paper. Even if you believe you can listen to a conversation and read the paper and/or watch the news at the same time, the appearance of giving your undivided attention conveys respect.

It shows that you care more about what your partner is saying than multi-tasking your mind. Make a conscious effort to ponder and reflect on the message, not the delivery. Focus your attention on the words, ideas, feelings, and underlying meaning.

## 5. Appreciate the emotion behind the words.

Do not focus just on the literal meaning of the words being said. Tune into the emotion behind the words and hear what is not being said.

What is not spoken is just as powerful and revealing as what is communicated.

## 6. Repeat what you heard.

A good way to make sure you have heard the conversation correctly and without preconceived ideas is to repeat what you believe your partner said to you. The purpose is to avoid hearing only what you want to hear and not miss crucial viewpoints. Everyone has filters that we use to hear information and this method helps keep the conversation focused on the present situation.

## 7. Don't be critical.

Hold your temper, be patient, and keep your emotions intact. Allow your partner enough time to finish his or her thoughts. You might find that what you were initially going to disagree with wasn't such a bad idea after all. Keep an open mind. By listening to another point of view, you might learn something new.

## 8. Ask questions.

Ask detailed questions that allow your partner to express and expand on his or her feelings and thoughts.

## 9. Be motivated to listen to one another.

If you are an unwilling listener, you will not be able to acquire effective communication skills. This is the person you love, and your partner deserves your quality time and attention more than anyone or anything. Your significant other is your main priority in life after God and deserves the respect of being listened to attentively.

# Chapter Eleven
## Barriers to Solving the Resolvable

### Maintaining a Positive Attitude, Selective Timing, and Mutual Respect

Attitude is the main barrier to resolving conflicts. Your manner is a reflection of the worth you place on yourself and your significant other. If you suppress your unresolved feelings of anger, resentment builds up and negatively affects longevity and balance.

If you do not air your grievances as soon as they arise, you will not be able to maintain the open, caring mind-set needed for genuine resolution of any situation that occurs.

Timing is the key to conflict resolution. Do not give in to the impulse to say the first thing that comes to your mind when you are angry. There is no need to bring to life each thought you verbalize, as they cannot be taken back once spoken. Take the time to calm down and compose yourself and decide what you want to say instead of attacking in the heat of the moment.

Many times conflicts that set you off are not really about the present circumstance, but a reaction to an event that happened long ago. Taking a moment to determine if you are overreacting to a minor situation is far better than saying something you may regret later. Once it is spoken, you cannot take back those words.

Trust is another vital component of effective conflict resolution. Once you have established mutual trust, you feel free to express your feelings openly without fear of retribution or abandonment. If there is no trust, effective conflict resolution cannot occur. Confidence as a couple allows substantive communication to happen. You know you love each other first and foremost.

## Airing Grievances

Burying issues and avoiding conflict and disagreements allows the seeds of resentment to take root and grow. Those couples who say they "never fight or disagree" are not living authentically. You will quarrel from time to time. But you can argue constructively without tearing each other apart.

Everyone has emotional buttons and those are pressed more in our intimate relationships, where we feel most vulnerable. It is important to express why you feel a certain way and freely discuss your reactions.

## Resolving Conflicts

All loving couples face conflicts, large and small. Our fantasy image of perfection usually does not include arguments. But the more prepared you are to face conflicts and acquire the skills to work through these inevitable issues, the faster you will resolve disagreements.

Harmony is achieved by learning how to resolve conflict in a constructive manner without allowing the disagreement to escalate to a shouting match and learning to compromise. If each of you must have your way on every issue that arises, you will not be together for long. A relationship cannot generate enough good feelings if the amount of time you spend on arguing exceeds the amount of time you are in agreement.

Pick your battles with discernment and refrain from trying to mold your partner into your ideal version of the perfect person. God is the potter, not you, and He designed your loved one in a specific manner for a predestined reason, just as He planned you. It is not your mission in life to take over God's job.

It can be difficult to remember how to communicate effectively during conflicts, so I encourage you to take the opportunity to explore how to resolve arguments when you are not in the middle of a battle.

These tools are a necessary part of maintaining balance. Your manner and voice tone are vital components to finding a mutually satisfying agreement, even if you end up agreeing to disagree.

The following are steps to take when faced with a conflict with your partner:

## *Identify and define the conflict.*

Focus on the matter at hand and stay in the present moment. Make a conscious effort to address issues when they occur. Avoid the tendency to allow your hurt or anger to fester internally and blow up at a later time.

If you allow yourself to hold on to anger, it will quickly turn into bitterness. You are definitely entitled to your feelings, but letting those emotions boil under the surface for an extended period of time is not spiritually responsible.

## *Agree to reach a resolution.*

Most of us take a fight-or-flight approach to conflict, sometimes only to make our point. Remember that you and your partner are on the same team and that you love each other. Dramatics will only extend the conflict period, cause unnecessary chaos, and deviate from the central problem.

When you agree to resolve an issue you acknowledge that both parties will compromise to reach a solution. It is not about one person getting his or her way and the other person caving in to manipulation or defeat.

You agree to air your differences and allow each other the opportunity to speak.

## *Explore your feelings.*

Ask yourself why you are so upset. Are you overreacting because one of your emotional buttons has been pushed? Explore your reaction and see if you are responding to the present situation or reliving a former episode.

If you are overreacting to a current incident because something triggered a previous painful event, tell your partner the history behind your emotions so he or she can better understand your reaction and can be sensitive to that area in the future.

## *Identify what you want.*

Don't be afraid to speak up. Your partner cannot give you what you want if you don't have the courage to ask for it. Relationships are driven by feelings, and it is your desire to reach that goal for each other.

Some people tend to be intimidated by arguments and become timid with their feelings. Their goal is to end the conflict quickly, even if they stifle their point of view and desires. Do not cave in to this behavior. It is not beneficial for you to accept a resolution you do not agree with out of fear.

## *Generate options and possible solutions.*

Be willing to back up your requests and desires with a solution that is mutually satisfactory. Sometimes we reject a new way of doing things simply because we have not thought of an alternative.

Be reasonable and fair in your request.

## *Choose mutual action.*

Resolving conflict does not mean taking on more responsibility because it is easier than arguing. A relationship is a partnership and if one person ends up with the responsibility for making it work, resentment will build up. One person is not assigned to exert all the effort while the relationship revolves around the other person's whims and desires. Everyone needs balance, boundaries, and defined roles.

## *Evaluate the outcome.*

If the first solution isn't a good fit, don't be afraid to revisit the issue and make changes. What seems doable in theory may be flawed in reality. Do not belittle your partner for having the courage to work for a better solution, as criticism will lead to avoidance when other issues arise.

The most important aspect of communicating during arguments is maintaining your awareness that you love each other despite the disagreement. The issues are not threatening your commitment or love.

## Thirty-Day Challenge

If you are currently in a committed relationship, you may already be in the habit of criticizing your partner. Many people feel compelled to point out every wrong thing their significant others do and all areas that need "fixing." This shows a tremendous lack of respect and drives a wedge in emotional intimacy.

My challenge to you is to go thirty days without saying anything negative to your partner, and finding one positive thing to say each day. Then tell someone about your daily positive affirmation of your partner. You will immediately see a positive change. In order to receive what we want from our partners, we must first give what we desire freely, openly, and willingly.

# Chapter Twelve
## Children

### Don't Compromise Your Desire to Have or Not Have Children

One of the most vital decisions you will make is whether or not to raise a family. Many women who want children stay with men who don't, perhaps because they already have children from a previous marriage.

The woman who stays in this type of situation believes that her significant other will eventually change his mind. But her childbearing years are passing by and the issue is still at an impasse.

If you and your partner agree to have children, you will find that the experience will add a new dimension, bringing a lifetime of opportunities for personal growth and deepening love.

Children will alter your routine as a couple and can enhance and intensify your commitment. They quickly bring to the surface any areas you have not resolved and push all your emotionally charged buttons.

They are a catalyst for change and growth. Sometimes this will be painful, but God can use these experiences to heal you.

### If I Stay Long Enough, He'll Change His Mind

To bring a child into the world is an awesome event. Each child is a blessing, a gift to you from God, and it will be your duty as a couple to raise that child in a stable environment to love and serve God. You will be obligated to instill good morals and values and lead by example.

When you are single, it is easy to get caught up with someone who seemingly has all the attributes you believe would make for a good match. If a man tells you that he does not want to have children, do not make the mistake of staying, with the idea that time will change his thinking. That is the situation Shannon is in. She believes she has found a man, who is a potential marriage partner, but she wants to have a baby and he does not.

*I'm dating a guy who is great: we have a good time together, we communicate well and lately we've been discussing larger issues like marriage and children. We are both in our 30's so it has been natural conversation even though it's only been a seven month relationship so far.*

*The problem is that he has never thought about having children. In fact, he was divorced from his first wife because of his feelings of having children of his own. I'm glad we discussed the issue because I do want at least one baby. He said he's been thinking about it a lot lately. He told me that, for him to even think about it, is good for me.*

*The conversation was a couple of weeks ago and I don't want to continually bring it up, which I haven't. He said he would think more about it. He tells me often that he's never felt the way he's feeling about me with another woman (other than his first wife).*

*What do I do? Do I give him a time limit?*
*How much time? I just don't want to in-*
*vest a couple years into this relationship*
*to find out he's decided no, he doesn't*
*want children. I really like him though*
*and I know he really likes me.*

The challenge is to be very aware of your goals and not be afraid to approach important topics that will determine your future together. Do not permit yourself to turn a blind eye to significant life objectives such as having children.

Raising a family requires a balance between God, husband and wife, and children. Both parents are responsible for the care, discipline, and love of the child, not just the mother. The most successful person in the world in the eyes of God is one who raises a godly child in an ungodly world. It is a privilege, a joy, a challenge, and a blessing to be called to nurture a child into maturity.

God's will for each couple is unique, fulfilling specific purposes to honor and glorify His name. Being in tune with God and listening to His voice, allowing Him to guide your steps as a couple and individually, will answer the question of whether to start a family or not. Not everyone is called to become a parent, and that's okay.

Child rearing can be a great source of contention. Therefore, it is important to discuss, before starting your family, what roles and responsibilities each of you will assume after children arrive.

Here are some options to consider:

- How many children do you want and how far apart in years?
- How do you envision your family functioning after a child is born?
- Will the mother stay home or work?
- What will be the role of the father in helping raise the child?

- What are your views regarding discipline and what role each parent will take?
- Are you in agreement that the father is the spiritual head of the household and is responsible for leading the children in learning about and loving God?

# ·Part Four Exercise·

It is your responsibility to learn how you need to receive love, which usually is the manner which you give love. You will find that your relationship partner gives and receives love in a different manner. I believe God brings us together with those who communicate love in ways out of our comfort zone so we can grow in understanding of one another.

The following are the most common ways people give and receive love:

## Language of Words of Affirmation

Verbal compliments
Words of praise
Words of appreciation
Focusing on positive qualities and characteristics
Bringing out the potential in your mate

## Language of Acts of Service

Mowing the yard
Taking care of the kids
Washing the car
Repairing the sink
Painting the bedroom

## Language of Receiving Gifts

Receiving flowers
Receiving cards
Receiving perfume/cologne

## Language of Physical Touch

Physical touch by taking the initiative – don't wait for them
Hugging
Holding hands
Sitting close
Kissing
Responsiveness in the bedroom

## Language of Quality Time

Spending time together
Meeting for lunch
Going on vacation
Spend time "connecting" daily
Doing what your partner likes to do
Listening to your partner

What language best describes the way you give and receive love?

In your past and/or current relationship, which language best describes the manner in which your partner gives and receives love?

How can you best communicate your need to receive love from your partner in the manner you most identify with?

What are the ways you can communicate your love to your partner in the manner he most identifies with?

# Part Five

# Marriage:
# The Ultimate Connection

In Part Five, Marriage: The Ultimate Connection you will read why marriage is the truest commitment choice you can make. You will also read how destructive living together is spiritually, emotionally and in some cases, physically.

Also outlined are the ways you can build your future marital foundation with strong pillars of mutual love, respect, honor, and belief in God.

# Chapter Thirteen
## The True Commitment Choice

## *Marriage is Not Just a Piece of Paper*

When you are single and without a significant other, there is a certain pinnacle of emotional and spiritual growth that you will reach through that experience. In a dating situation, sharing mutual love, building a solid foundation for your friendship, and strengthening the bond will plateau at some point.

When you have made a commitment to stand before God, family, and friends and declare your love through the union of marriage, spiritual evolution will escalate as you mature together as a couple and in your mutual walk with God.

All the elements involved in planning for the ceremony solidify the ultimate pledge of love. As a couple, you are broadcasting your intention to spend your life together and asking God for His blessing.

Marriage is the ultimate promise, and it greatly differs from living together. Really, there is no comparison. When you live together without the vows of marriage, at least one person is emotionally uncommitted. Marriage is not just a piece of paper. No matter how married you "feel" living together is not the same type of union as marriage.

Society implies that living together is empowering for women. The reality is that this type of situation places women in a vulnerable position. Living together may provide a woman with a better lifestyle than she is able to experience alone.

But when cohabitation ends, the woman is usually the one who will be left with little material possessions to her name. There are limited recourses for women in cohabitation arrangements, and the only legal steps available to her require that the couple presented themselves to society as married. Most cohabitating couples do not give others that impression.

God did not create women to feel weak and powerless against men. Women are complements to men and should be treated with the love and respect God intended.

By following the word of society instead of the Word of God, you set yourself up for emotional pain. What is more powerful than seeing yourself as God sees you?

## What's the Harm in a Trial Relationship?

There are biblical reasons for couples not to live together before marriage. Over time cohabitation causes emotional and spiritual damage to each individual.

Confusion, pain, and heartache are common results for the person who wants to get married. (Usually there is one person who wants to get married and one who doesn't—at least not to the person he or she is living with.) Friends and family who open their hearts to the couple also suffer when they decide to go their separate ways.

Society views cohabitation as a practical and rational way for a couple to try out their relationship. The reasoning is that emotional and financial hardship can be avoided if the couple finds they cannot live together. Couples ask, "Why go through the time, expense, and fuss of a wedding ceremony if we don't know if we'll be compatible?" But cohabitation is not an equal comparison to marriage.

Living together cheapens intimacy and carries consequences. Love without commitment is lust. Marriage provides security from the fear of being used, seduced, and abandoned.

Some of the consequences of living together include misplaced trust, unplanned pregnancy, disease, and emotional issues that can last a lifetime. Society glamorizes sex and creates the perception that sex outside of marriage is not only acceptable, but expected.

Many people engage in sex not because they want to but because they feel obligated to "prove" their love to their partner. The pressure to conform to the "anything goes" attitude of secular sexual activity is enormous.

If a person wants to hold on to his or her virginity and wait until marriage, society views this as a novelty, certainly far from the norm. But in God's eyes, the person who waits for marriage is the standard.

## Living Together Is Not Divorce Prevention

Living together is not marriage preparation but divorce training. Living together increases the likelihood of divorce if the couple later decides to marry. The National Survey of Families and Households found that couples who cohabit before marriage are 50 percent more likely to divorce.[iv] For example, among women aged between 40 and 50 years, who married when they were in their early twenties (20-24 years) and who cohabited before marriage, 39% were divorced compared to 21% of those who did not. The ratio of divorce between couples who pre-maritally cohabited and couples who did not cohabit, is 1.8 to 1, showing an 80% greater likelihood of divorce among those who cohabited before marriage.

People who have multiple cohabiting relationships before marriage are more likely to experience marital conflict, marital unhappiness and eventual divorce than people who do not cohabit before marriage.

Researchers attribute some but not all of these differences to the differing characteristics of people who cohabit, the so-called "selection effect," rather than to the experience of cohabiting itself. It has been hypothesized that the negative effects of cohabitation on future marital success may diminish as living together becomes a common experience among today's young adults. However, according to one recent study of couples who were married between 1981 and 1997, the negative effects persist among younger groups, supporting the view that the cohabitation experience itself contributes to problems in marriage.[v]

The same survey also found that unmarried couples living together are twice as likely to be unhappy in their relationships as are those who are married.

Many studies have found that those who live together before marriage have a considerably higher chance of eventually divorcing. The reasons for this are not well understood. In part, the type of people who are willing to live together may also be those who are more willing to divorce.

There is some evidence that the act of cohabitation itself generates attitudes in people that are more conducive to divorce, for example the attitude that relationships are temporary and easily can be ended.[vi]

Information collected by the General Household Survey allows divorce rates by duration of marriage to be estimated for couples in their first marriage. From this data the probability of a marriage ending in divorce or separation can be calculated for both those who cohabited premaritally and those who did not. According to an article in Population Trends the results are clear cut: 'For every duration of marriage, the cumulative proportions of marriages which had broken down are higher amongst marriages in which there was premarital cohabitation than amongst marriages in which there was no premarital cohabitation.'

Among people who have divorced, the prevalence of cohabiting before a second marriage has always been higher than before first. There is a greater the proportion of men and women who premaritally cohabit before their second marriage. So the idea that premarital cohabitation reduces the likelihood of an unhappy marriage is false.

## Cohabitation is Unsafe

• According to the National Crime Victimization Survey, of all violent crimes against women by their intimate partners between 1979 and 1987, about 65 percent were committed by either a boyfriend or ex-husband, while only 9 percent were committed by their husbands.[vii]

• Another study, published in the Journal of Family Violence, explains the following regarding the association between batterer and victim, "The most frequently cited relationship was cohabitation, with close to one-half (48 percent) of the couples living together."[viii]

• The Family Violence Research Program at the University of New Hampshire conducted a study of more than two thousand adults concerning this subject. It was concluded that the overall rates of violence for cohabiting couples was twice as high and the overall rate for "severe" violence was nearly five times as high for cohabiting couples when compared with married couples.[ix]

• "Aggression is at least twice as common among cohabiters as it is among married partners," states yet another expert, Dr. Jan E. Stets, in a major study comparing cohabitational and marital aggression. In a one year period, 35 out of every 100 cohabiting couples have experienced some form of physical aggression, compared to 15 out of every 100 married couples. The lowest percent was found among married couples at 19 percent.[x]

• A study published by the University of Chicago found that of women who had reportedly been forced to perform a sexual act, 46 percent reported that the aggressor was someone they were in love with but not married to, while only 9 percent reported that the aggressor was a spouse.[xi]

• When it comes to hitting, shoving, and throwing things, cohabitating couples are more than three times more likely than married couples to say things get that far out of hand.[xii]

## Why is Cohabitation Unsafe?

What makes live-in relationships so comparatively violent?

There are two main factors. First, it has been found that cohabiters are less likely to be connected to a network of family or friends who can serve to hold the couple accountable for their behavior toward each other.[xiii] This can contribute to a feeling of isolation and anonymity in committing acts of violence against a mate. Without a community of support, a woman feels she has no place to turn when her cohabitational relationship becomes abusive.

Secondly, people entering cohabiting relationships show greater tendencies toward individualism, leading to a strong desire for self-autonomy within the relationship.[xiv] One of the appeals of cohabitation is the increased freedom and decreased responsibility to a mate.

However, a David Popenoe study reveals a stark difference between how a cohabiting man and woman view their relationship. A woman in a cohabiting relationship tends to see moving in with her mate as a step towards marriage, while a man tends to regard the relationship as more of a sexual opportunity without the ties of long-term commitment.[xv]

If a woman views a live-in relationship as the next step toward marriage, and a cohabiting man sees himself as a single person in a live-in but non-committed relationship, great potential exists for conflict to develop over defining relationship boundaries. Too often in cohabiting relationships, conflict escalates into violence.

It is this sense of being bound that helps stabilize love. The couple who is firmly committed to marriage has a much greater chance of a genuine lasting relationship than the couple who regards their living arrangement as a trial period subject to termination.

Marriage makes you try harder. It forces you to open yourself up and expose your vulnerabilities, compromise each day, and practice what you preach. Your spouse holds you accountable for your words and actions. You have someone who will be truthful with you. And together, with God as the center of your marriage, you can be set free.

## You Are Worthy of Marriage

I encourage you not to despair about previous relationship choices. The clock cannot be turned back from what has already happened. But you can start over right now by making a commitment to God to treat yourself as royalty.

With Jesus as your Savior, you are an heir to the kingdom of God. Your body is a sacred shrine, created in the image of God. Your empowerment comes from being mindful of how priceless your gift of love is, emotionally and physically.

You need to make a conscious decision to protect yourself by being selective with who you allow in your life. You are not required to share your gifts with every person who wants a sample. You never need to "prove" your love physically before marriage.

H. Norman Wright, a prominent Christian marriage counselor, notes the benefits of waiting until marriage to live together:

1. No guilt (of having offended God).

2. No fear (of having to build a marriage on an unexpected pregnancy).

3. No comparison (of the spouse with a previous "live-in").

4. Spiritual growth (in placing physical desires under Christ and in developing self-control).

5. Greater joy (in fulfilling that which is saved for the marriage relationship).[xvi]

A key asset of marriage is the vow of permanence, which allows spouses to develop and handle challenges together. When you are single, you must accomplish all of life's tasks alone, but in marriage each partner can choose what needs to be done, according to that person's strengths.

When you marry, the public declaration changes the way you think about yourself, the way you act and think about the future, and how others treat you.

# Chapter Fourteen
# Making God Your Marital
# Foundation

## God Blesses Marriages Surrendered to His Authority

Marriage is a sacred experience, comprising a trinity between God, husband, and wife. Marriage permits you to grow emotionally by facing unresolved feelings and choosing to get beyond them. Marriage also allows you to grow spiritually in your faith in God. Love based on the soul and spirit has a life of its own.

Mutual core beliefs are vital to the lasting survival of your relationship. God has a structure and design for marriage. Our society perpetuates the myth that women can have it all (powerful career and family) and do it all well. When women try to achieve both goals concurrently, they usually end up giving up one of God's greatest gifts—an adoring husband and children—in the pursuit of money, position, power, and recognition.

Many women sacrifice their childbearing years in order to pursue a career, only to wake up years later wondering what happened to their lives. Yes, women are capable of achieving academic excellence, running corporations successfully, and having their own businesses. But all these quests come with an extremely high price that many realize only later in life.

A recent *Harvard Business Review* article entitled *"Executive Women and the Myth of Having It All"*[xvii] revealed that when it comes to having a high-powered career and a family, the painful truth is that women in the United States don't "have it all." At midlife, in fact, at least a third of the country's high-achieving women — a category that includes high wage earners across a variety of professions — do not have children. For many, this wasn't a conscious choice. Indeed, most yearn for motherhood.

So finds economist Sylvia Ann Hewlett, who recently fielded a nation-wide survey to explore the professional and private lives of highly educated and high-earning women. Many professional women who are also raising children have suffered insurmountable career setbacks. Hewlett's data show that, for many women, the demands of ambitious careers, the asymmetries of male-female relationships, and the difficul-ties of conceiving later in life undermine the possibility of combining high-level work with family. By contrast, Hewlett's research reveals that high-achieving men continue to "have it all."

Of the men she surveyed, 79 percent report wanting children, and 75 percent have them. Indeed, the more successful the man, the more likely he is to have a spouse and children. The opposite holds true for women. Recognizing that changes won't happen overnight, Hewlett exhorts young women to be more deliberate about their career and family choices. It is imperative that women lead a purposeful life, focused on God's will and mindful of the paths they select.

At this point in your life you may not be contemplating marriage in the immediate future, but I assure you that it is important to start forming your ideals now. It is my experience through my work with others that the sooner you have an idea of the kind of marriage you want – with the type of person you desire to share life with, the easier it will be for you to manifest exactly that life.

Because we all are so inundated with images of what the world deems "a perfect marriage", I decided to show you what the Bible reveals about marriage and our relationship roles. Many couples end up living an unfulfilled, empty life together because they were not paying attention to the important aspects of their relationship. They allowed their senses to dictate their course and find themselves truly living in the world, ruled by society's view of "normal."

The key to a lasting and loving marriage is growing together in faith, building a solid foundation for your love to mature spiritually and emotionally.

## Biblical Structure and Roles in Marriage

God has a structure for marriage. It is a matter of rank and order. With societal roles of men and women so fluid, and the struggle couples have defining what is a "fair" role in their marriage, it is important to get back to the truth and follow God's plan for marriage.

He created men with an innate desire to protect and lead. He created women with an intrinsic desire to be closer to Him.

The Bible teaches that God has imposed structure in all major human relationships by creating offices of authority (state, work, family, marriage). He does this to restrain anarchy and provide social order in a world where people are inclined to do their own will rather than follow God's will.

He knows this structure can be abused and He condemns that abuse. However, this structure is preferable to having no foundation at all. And this is the case in marriage as well as other interactions we have, even though there are significant differences in the way each of these offices function.

So what does structure look like in a biblical marriage? Contrary to what you may have heard, it is not chauvinistic.

It is very different from the secular preconceived notions of an archaic structure that dehumanizes and declasses women.

## Biblical Marriage Structure Myths

First, let's look at some of the most common beliefs that society has about marriages with biblical foundations. Then we will review what the Bible truly says so we can dispute those incorrect notions.

## Myth 1: Men are superior to women.

> *So God created people in his own image; God patterned them after himself; male and female he created them.*
> *Genesis 1:27(AMP)*

As seen in the above passage, the Bible teaches that men and women are equal in their essential identity. Our identity as a person created in the image of God is different from the marital roles God has designated to men and women.

The husband plays his role as head of the family in marriage. But that does not make him superior any more than a policeman directing traffic is superior to the driver on the road. The policeman simply outranks the driver on the road.

God is the Creator of the universe and has the ultimate master plan for your life and mine. He made Adam first by design. Women were created to complement men. In essence, man, as a groom, is a type of Christ. The groom represents Jesus, who marches into battle for the bride. He fights to protect her and his family.

In marriage, God has designated the husband as the spiritual head of the household. It is his responsibility to lead the way for spiritual growth, focus, and commitment to living a godly, Christian life. The husband is responsible for blessing his wife and children. Woman, as a bride, symbolizes the church. The bride takes direction from the groom. By honoring our roles in the union of marriage and our responsibilities toward each other to make it work, we obey God's will for our marriage.

Some women believe that if they follow the biblical marriage structure, they will become servants to their husbands, at the mercy of the man's choices and whims. As head of the household, a husband has a responsibility not to abuse his God-given power.

A husband should exercise his decision-making authority when an impasse arises in major, life-changing decisions. If after careful and prayerful discussion husband and wife cannot agree, the husband should assume the responsibility to make the decision that he thinks will best advance God's glory and the family's good.

This does not mean the husband is exempt from the necessary art of compromise in a loving and mutually respectful marriage. He cannot use his authority to manipulate his spouse and to get his way on every issue.

In a mutually revered marriage, the couple can normally come to an agreement about the best course of action in most situations. But when a couple reaches an impasse on a significant decision, the husband is responsible for selecting the best path to follow.

God calls on wives to respect their husbands' position and go along with a good attitude with his choice.

## Myth 2: Wives should never correct their husbands.

*Let the words of Christ, in all their richness, live in your hearts and make you wise. Use his words to teach and counsel each other. Sing psalms and hymns and spiritual songs to God with thankful hearts.* *Colossians 3:16(NLT)*

The Bible insists on mutual subjection within the marriage. It states that Christian husbands should be ready to receive instruction and admonition from their wives.

A marriage is a partnership with distinct roles and responsibilities within its structure. A distinct marital role does not mean one partner is a spectator, excused from participation.

## Myth 3: Wives should obey their husbands.

*And further, you will submit to one another out of reverence for Christ. You wives will submit to your husbands as you do to the Lord. For a husband is the head of his wife as Christ is the head of his body, the church; he gave his life to be her Savior. As the church submits to Christ, so you wives must submit to your husbands in everything.* *Ephesians 5:21-24(NLT)*

This concept is contentious because, when taken out of context, it gives some people the impression that women must be subservient to their husbands. This verse is not advocating men to rule over their wives, nor is it about women losing their voices and roles. It simply addresses rank and authority in the structure of marriage.

The final expression of being filled with the Spirit is "submitting to one another" because Christ is one's Lord. In Ephesians, the apostle Paul clearly shows that Christians are a new social order, created to express the fullness of Christ in the midst of the old, fallen order. The Holy Spirit empowers Christians to exist in relationship with one another in a radical, culturally transforming way; namely, through mutual self-submission.

The ground for this radically new approach to human relationships is "out of reverence for Christ." The reason for that awe is the radical nature of Christ's earthly life, the total, free submission of Himself as God's suffering servant, climaxed in His self-giving on the cross. Reverence and awe toward that self-giving love is to motivate our mutual self-submission to one another.

So the injunction to submit for wives—as for all believers—is based on freedom, not authority.

The submission of the wife to the husband is to be "as to the Lord." It is not to be expected as a matter of course by the cultural norms enforced upon women, who were seen as inferior to males in both Jewish and Gentile cultures. No, her submission is to be freely chosen, being there for her partner "as to the Lord"; that is, as a disciple of the Lord, as one who follows in His servant footsteps, motivated by self-giving love. This kind of submission is not a reinforcement of traditional norms; it is a fundamental challenge to secular society.

## Myth 4: Wives should stay at home.

The Bible holds the raising of godly children in very high regard and opposes the current sentiment that women who choose to quit their careers to focus full time on their children are second-class citizens or not doing a "real" job.

The Bible also affirms wives as active workers in the church and in the work world. An example can be found in Proverbs 31, as the words of King Lemuel reveal the legacy his mother taught him.

## Myth 5: Husbands may use their authority to get what they want.

> But I have no right to say who will sit on the thrones next to mine. God has prepared those places for the ones he has chosen." When the ten other disciples discovered what James and John had asked, they were indignant. So Jesus called them together and said, "You know that in this world kings are tyrants, and officials lord it over the people beneath them. But among you it should be quite different. Whoever wants to be a leader among you must be your servant, and whoever wants to be first must be the slave of all. For even I, the Son of Man, came here not to be served but to serve others, and to give my life as a ransom for many." *Mark 10:40-45(NLT)*

Jesus specifically forbade this abuse of authority in His teachings and furthermore, Paul calls on husbands to imitate Jesus by using their authority to sacrificially serve their wives.

> *And you husbands must love your wives with the same love Christ showed the church. He gave up his life for her.* Ephesians 5:25(NLT)

In the same way, husbands must give honor to wives. They are to treat them with understanding. A woman may be physically weaker than the man, but she is the equal partner in God's eyes. If your future husband does not treat you as he should, his prayers will not be heard by God.

The husband's submission is to express itself in the kind of radical self-giving love that Christ demonstrated when "he gave himself up for" the church. For that is the way Christ loved the church, and husbands, like their wives, are to be imitators of Christ.

A husband is blessed by God as head of the household; however, leadership is not a privilege to be abused. The responsibility lies in initiating serving love.

The submission of wives to husbands is not about obedience, but about respect and humility. And these characteristics are self-chosen moral goals to be sought after by all who seek to emulate the self-giving nature of Jesus.

# Chapter Fifteen
## Guidelines for a Loving Relationship

## Positive Feelings, Mutual Respect, Daily Kindness, and Affection

Everyone wants to feel special, especially in love, and one of the best ways to make your boyfriend or girlfriend feel exceptional is to communicate admiration to him or her. There are many ways couples can show each other the esteem they deserve within the relationship. Couples who pay attention to the small things that strengthen a bond over time will be successful in deepening their connection with each other and their mutual bond with God.

### How Can I Show My Respect?

#### Maintain mutual trust.

The integrity of your relationship depends on mutual trust. In order to feel safe, secure, and accepted, trust must be protected. Discuss areas where you feel vulnerable and how your partner can alleviate those fears and strengthen trust.

Do not allow outside acquaintances and friends to dance around the area of an emotional affair. A commitment includes being faithful to one another physically, emotionally, and spiritually.

## *Stay in touch with each other's lives.*

It is easy to fall into a routine where you share superficial information concerning your day and then zone out in front of the television. Make it a priority to go beyond the trivial and connect emotionally and spiritually.

A relationship is a process of daily and continuous growth. We evolve each day, and what was true about ourselves one day may not be true the next week. Allow yourself to stay in the present and let go of the urge to keep each other static.

## *Pray together.*

This builds intimacy in your mutual walk with God. Praying together deepens your commitment to His divine will for your lives and submission to that will. Together you agree in prayer to trust God's plan for your lives. Shared prayer allows you to stay spiritually connected. The power of praying for one another during times of need is most powerful when it comes from your loved one.

Praise God each day and bless each other each day. Truly committed people walk together in faith. By praying together, you provide an armor as a couple as you follow Christ and live lives of practiced kindness, goodness, and mercy. When you pray together you open the door to sharing your ideas about God.

## *Advise each other.*

Your significant other is your best resource in many areas as he or she is your best confidant. Asking for advice communicates respect. Truth is freedom. Be reliable, gentle, and courteous. Do not deceive each other. Have integrity in your thoughts, words, and actions.

## *Be open to correction.*

No one is flawless, although we may place enormous pressure on ourselves to be the picture perfect person. When areas that need correction are pointed out, look for the truth in what he or she is saying instead of looking for the flaws to discredit the message. It is easy to buy into the prideful lie that if you receive correction, you will lose respect. In most cases nothing could be further from the truth.

## *Express your love tangibly.*

Love your each other by expressing your feelings in ways that help him or her feel special. The small, daily signs of affection, loving actions, and words of endearment, inclusion, appreciation, and attention are tangible ways for couples to express their affection for each other on a daily basis, to keep the emotional connection alive.

Each relationship has its own character. This uniqueness invites couples to discover and live the love of God through the love of their partners. A lasting union is built on a foundation of godly love, but it also needs daily doses of acknowledgment of your adoration for each other.

## *Focus on correcting your own flaws.*

The only person you can change is yourself. By becoming a better person and not focusing on improving the other person, you will positively influence one another. Our vulnerabilities are exposed in relationships which places our unresolved issues in the spotlight.

God says we should concentrate on improving ourselves, which will give us peace instead of anxiety, anger, and depression. This spotlight will result in the best influence for godly change.

By learning to appreciate and respect each other for the persons God made each of you to be, you begin centering on the good qualities and characteristics instilled in your partner.

## *Turn to Christ for your deepest needs.*

Love is not primarily a feeling; it is a choice to serve sacrificially (even when it is costly to do so) and freely (without expectation of return). The problem is that we are very needy people, and we naturally tend to look to our relationship partners to meet our desires. Only knowing God and surrendering to His will for your life will fulfill your deepest wants.

He is our resource that enables us to serve each other sacrificially. We need to receive Christ, cultivate a mind-set focused on what we have in Him, and learn how to depend on Him to empower us and show us how to love others. Then we can be grateful and not demanding when God expresses His love to us through our significant others. We can serve freely.

# Conclusion

It is my hope that after completing this book you now have a clear picture of a healthy, loving and spiritually connected relationship and most importantly, discovered your bond with God. When you find the love of your life and make the decision to marry, you will be inspired to accomplish more, love abundantly and share yourself openly and sincerely with others. You are not fearful of being vulnerable with others.

The love and support of my husband has brought peace and fulfillment to my life. The insight my marriage provides opens my heart to higher levels of growth. I know that I can accomplish all things through Jesus Christ because He is my Savior. I am incredibly blessed to do God's will each day and share that joy with my husband.

There is no substitute for marrying the person God has selected for you. That person is waiting for you to let go of your façade so your true self can be clearly seen. Your job is to trust God and His timing. Be ready to accept the blessing of this gift when it arrives.


It will happen to you.

[i] Eleanor Roosevelt, *This Is My Story*, (Garden City Publishing Co., 1939).

[ii] Abraham Harold Maslow, *Toward a Psychology of Being* (Wiley, 1998).

[iii] Clay Tucker-Ladd, *Psychological Self-Help* (Clayton Tucker-Ladd & Mental Health Net, 1996).

[iv] Claire M. Kamp Dush, Catherine L. Cohan, and Paul R. Amato, "The Relationship between Cohabitation and Marital Quality and Stability: Change Across Cohorts?" *Journal of Marriage and the Family*, 2003, 65: 539-49.
David Popenoe and Barbara Dafoe Whitehead, *Should We Live Together*, 2nd Ed. (New Brunswick, NJ: The National Marriage Project, Rutgers University, 2002).
William G. Axinn and Jennifer S. Barber, "Living Arrangements and Family Formation Attitudes in Early Adulthood," *Journal of Marriage and the Family*, 59 1997, 595-611.
William J. Axinn and Arland Thornton, "The Relationship Between Cohabitation and Divorce: Selectivity or Causal Influence," *Demography*, 29-3, 1992, 357-374.
Robert Schoen "First Unions and the Stability of First Marriages," *Journal of Marriage and the Family*, 1992, 54: 281-84.


v From the National Marriage Project's Ten Things to Know series, David Popenoe and Barbara Dafoe Whitehead. Research: See discussion in Claire M. Kamp Dush, Catherine L. Cohan, and Paul R. Amato, "The Relationship between Cohabitation and Marital Quality and Stability: Change Across Cohorts?" Journal of Marriage and the Family 65 (August 2003): 539-49. For a comprehensive review of the research on the relationship between cohabitation and risk of marital disruption, see David Popenoe and Barbara Dafoe Whitehead, Should We Live Together?, 2nd Ed. (New Brunswick, NJ: The National Marriage Project, Rutgers University, 2002). See also William G. Axinn and Jennifer S. Barber, "Living Arrangements and Family Formation Attitudes in Early Adulthood," Journal of Marriage and the Family 59 1997), 595-611; William J. Axinn and Arland Thornton, "The Relationship Between Cohabitation and Divorce: Selectivity or Causal Influence," Demography 29-3 (1992), 357-374; Robert Schoen, "First Unions and the Stability of First Marriages," Journal of Marriage and the Family 54 (1992), 281-84. However, living together with the person one intends to marry does not increase the risk of divorce. For first-time cohabiting couples who eventually marry, living together is linked to the engagement process. See, for example, Jay Teach-man, "Premarital Sex, Premarital Cohabitation and the Risk of Subsequent Marital Dissolution Among Women," Journal of Marriage and the Family 65 (May 2003), 444-455; Susan L. Brown and Alan Booth, "Cohabitation versus Marriage: A Comparison of Relationship Quality," Journal of Marriage and the Family 58 (1996), 668-678

vi Alfred DeMaris and K. Vaninadha Rao, "Premarital Cohabitation and Marital Instability in the United States: A Reassessment" *Journal of Marriage and the Family* 54 (1992), 178-190; Pamela J. Smock, "Cohabitation in the United States," *Annual Review of Sociology* 26 (2000).

vii "Criminal Victimization in the United States, 1992," US Department of Justice, Office of Justice Programs, Bureau of Justice Statistics (March 1994), NCJ-145125, p. 31.
viii Albert R. Roberts, "Psychosocial Characteristics of Batterers: A Study of 234 Men Charged with Domestic Violence Offences," *Journal of Family Violence*, 2 (1987), 81-93.

ix Kersti Yllo and Murray A. Straus, "Interpersonal Violence among Married and Cohabiting Couples," *Family Relations* 30 (1981), 339-347.

x Jan E. Stets, "Cohabiting and Marital Aggression: The Role of Social Isolation, "*Journal of Marriage and the Family*, 53 (1991), 669-680.

xi Edward O. Laumann, John H. Gagnon, Robert T. Michael, and Stuart Michaels, *The Social Organization of Sexuality: Sexual Practices in the United States* (Chicago: University of Chicago Press, 1994), p. 225.

xii Linda J. Waite and Maggie Gallagher, *The Case For Marriage* (New York: Doubleday, 2000), p. 155.

xiii Jan E. Stets and Murray A. Straus, "The Marriage License as a Hitting License: A Comparison of Assaults in Dating, Cohabiting, and Married Couples," *Journal of Family Violence*, 4 (1989), 161-180.

xiv Jan E. Stets and Murray A. Straus, "The Marriage License as a Hitting License: A Comparison of Assaults in Dating, Cohabiting, and Married Couples," *Journal of Family Violence*, 4 (1989), 161-180.

[xv] Steven E. Rhoads, *Taking Sex Differences Seriously* (San Francisco: Encounter Books, 2004), p. 113.

[xvi] H. Norman Wright, *Finding Your Perfect Mate* (Harvest House Publishers, January, 2003).

[xvii] Sylvia Ann Hewlett, "Executive Women and the Myth of Having It All," *Harvard Business Review* , April 1, 2002.

Printed in the United States
62598LVS00004B/77

9 781931 947183